THE USBORNE
SPOTTER'S GUIDE
BIRDS, FLOWERS
AND TREES

PART ONE
BIRDS

Cover designed by Stephen Wright and Lucy Smith

Series designer: Laura Fearn

First published in 2001 by Usborne Publishing Limited, Usborne House,
83-85 Saffron Hill, London EC1N 8RT, England.
www.usborne.com

Printed in Spain

Golden
eagle

CONTENTS

Written by Peter Holden – Head of the Youth and Volunteers Department, the Royal Society for the Protection of Birds
Illustrated by Trevor Boyer
Designed by Susannah Owen and Cristina Adami
Edited by Felicity Brooks, Sue Jacquemier and Sue Tarsky
Photographs © Digital Vision
Additional illustrations by Chris Shields

HOW TO USE PART ONE

Part one of this book will help you to identify many of the birds of Britain, Ireland and other parts of Europe. The pictures show birds perching, swimming or flying, depending on how that kind of bird is most often seen.

As well as a colour picture, each bird also has a description to help you to identify it. The pictures are not drawn to scale, but the description gives you the average length of the bird from its beak to its tail.

Kingfisher 17cm

The measurements in this book show how long a bird would be if it were stretched out like this

Buzzards are most often seen in flight

Partridges are most often seen on the ground

Shovelers are usually seen swimming

4

Each bird's description tells you where to look for the bird. Beside each picture is a small, blank circle. Each time you spot that bird, make a tick in the circle. The example below shows how the birds are drawn and described in this book.

← HOOPOE
Rare visitor to Britain, seen mainly in spring. More common in southern Europe. Probes ground for insects with its long bill. 28cm.

Circle for ticking

WHAT LIVES WHERE
The green area on this map shows the part of Europe that is covered by this book. Not every bird from each country is in the book, and some are not found everywhere in the green area. The descriptions refer to the British Isles, unless another area is named.

British Isles

Europe

WHERE TO WATCH BIRDS

Birds are everywhere, which makes watching them a good hobby. You can start by watching them from a window in your home, or in a garden. If there are only a few birds, try putting out food and water to attract more (see pages 55-56).

When you can identify all the birds near your home, try looking in a local park. School playing fields, old gravel pits and even rubbish tips also attract birds. Always take an adult with you and make sure that you stay safe at all times.

Lakes, ponds and streams are home to ducks, swans, rails and wading birds such as herons. Dippers and wagtails visit fast-flowing streams.

Seashores, cliffs and estuaries attract many species, especially at low tide when birds come to feed. Rocky cliffs provide nest sites.

Each different kind of bird is called a species. You will be able to see new species whenever you visit new habitats (places where birds live). The photos on these pages show habitats where you may see a wide range of species.

WHAT TO TAKE

When you go out to spot birds, wear comfortable clothes and shoes, suitable for outdoors. Take this book and a notepad and pencil so that you can make notes and sketches to record what you see.

As you do more birdwatching, you will probably want to use binoculars. Visit a good shop and try out several pairs. The best sizes are 8x30 or 8x40 (never more than 10x50 or they will be too heavy).

Forests provide nest sites, shelter and food for many birds. Conifers are home to fewer birds than broadleef trees.

Make sure your binoculars are light enough to carry around with you.

WHAT TO LOOK FOR

When you are trying to identify a bird, ask yourself these questions: What size and shape is it? What colour is it? Does it have any special markings? Where does it live? How does it feed? How does it fly?

Remember that in some cases the males and females of a species look different from each other. In this book these symbols are used to show which is which:

♂ = Male

♀ = Female

Be aware that some species have different plumages (feathers) in summer and winter.

Ruff in summer

Ruff in winter

Female chaffinch

♀

Male chaffinch ♂

Juvenile ringed plover

Adult ringed plover

Also remember that the young birds (juveniles) of some species look different from the adults.

THE PARTS OF A BIRD

Although birds vary from species to species, they all have wings, feathers and a beak. To describe birds accurately, it's useful to know the names of some of their other parts too.

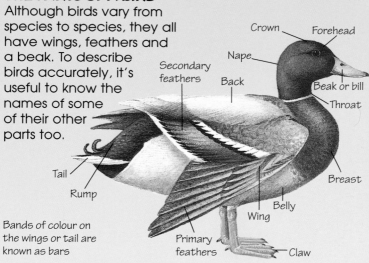

Male mallard

Crown
Forehead
Nape
Secondary feathers
Back
Beak or bill
Throat
Tail
Rump
Breast
Belly
Wing
Primary feathers
Claw

Bands of colour on the wings or tail are known as bars

NOTES AND SKETCHES

Try to make sketches of the birds you spot and note down when and where you saw them and what the weather was like. Estimate the length of the bird, or compare it to the size of one you know. Write down its shape and colour, and what it sounds like.

Here are some notes that an expert bird watcher might make.

Date/Time: 11.6.2001 9.35am
Place: Baxford Lake
Habitat: open water with shallow edges, grassy banks with a few trees
Weather: hazy sun, light breeze
Description: duck feeding from surface of water or just below it by up-ending. 1 of group of 5 ducks. 2 different plumages - could be males and females
Size: slightly larger than nearby coot, much smaller than a swan
Plumage: head dark green, body two-tone grey, breast chestnut. White ring round neck. Beak yellowy-green. Tail black and white with curly black feathers on top. Legs orange
Shape: typical duck shape
Voice: loud quacks, quiet nasal calls
Conclusion: a male mallard?

SPOTTING RARE BIRDS

Some of the birds in this book may not be very common where you live. Try to spot them if you go away on holiday or on a trip away from home.

Other birds are rare in the wild. You can tick off rare birds if you spot them at a bird reserve or a bird sanctuary, or if you see them on television.

Coasts are good places to see birds, but you should never try to climb cliffs and rocks or cross mud flats. It can be very dangerous.

SHAG, GANNET, CORMORANT

Crest only in nesting season

◀ SHAG

Lives near the sea. Nests in colonies on rocky coasts. Dives for fish. Young are brown. 78cm.

Shags fly low, close to water

▼ GANNET

Lives and nests on sea cliffs. Plunges from high up, head first, into water to catch fish. 92cm.

▶ CORMORANT

Seen near the sea but also at inland lakes. Some have grey head and neck in breeding season. Nests in colonies. 92cm.

White patch in breeding season

GEESE

➡ BRENT GOOSE
Look for this small, dark goose on estuaries in winter. 58cm.

Brent goose

Canada geese were brought here from N. America

⬅ CANADA GOOSE
A large, noisy goose. Look in parks. Nests wild in Britain. 95cm.

➡ GREYLAG GOOSE
Nests wild in Scotland. Others have been released further south. Wild birds from Iceland visit Scotland in winter. 82cm.

Barnacle goose has more white on head than Canada goose

⬅ BARNACLE GOOSE
Look for Barnacle geese on the west coasts of Britain and Ireland in winter. Feeds in flocks on farmland. 63cm.

12

GEESE, SWANS

➡ PINK-FOOTED GOOSE
A winter visitor. Seen in large numbers on fields in Scotland and near coasts in England. 68cm.

⬅ BEAN GOOSE
A rare winter visitor from northern Europe. Grazes on farmland away from the coast. 80cm.

➡ WHITE-FRONTED GOOSE
A winter visitor to estuaries, marshes and farmland. Look for white at base of bill. 72cm.

Mute swan 152cm

Whooper swan 152cm

Bewick's swan 122cm

⬅ SWANS
Mute swans are often seen in parks or on rivers. The others come to Britain in winter and can be seen on lakes or flooded fields.

13

DUCKS

Mallard   Teal   Wigeon

♀

♂

← MALLARD
Found near most inland waters. Only the female gives the familiar "quack". 58cm.

○

→ TEAL
Smallest European duck. A very shy bird. It prefers the shallow edges of lakes. Flies with fast wing beats. 35cm.

○

♀

♂

♂

♀

← WIGEON
Sometimes seen grazing on fields near water. Form flocks in winter especially near the sea. Male's call is a loud "wheeo". 46cm.

○

→ PINTAIL
Uses its long neck to feed on plants under the water. Look for these birds in winter, often near the sea. 66cm.

○

♀

♂

14

Pintail Shoveler Pochard Tufted duck Eider

➡ SHOVELER
Likes quiet lakes and shallow water. Uses its long, flat bill to filter food from the surface of the water Call is a low "quack". 51cm.

♀

♂

♀

♂

◀ POCHARD
Spends much of its time resting on open water. Dives for food. More likely to be seen in winter. 46cm.

➡ TUFTED DUCK
Diving duck which is more common in winter. Can sometimes be seen on park lakes. 43cm.

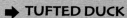

♀

♂

♂

♀

◀ EIDER
Breeds around rocky northern coasts. Forms large flocks on the sea in winter. 58cm.

DUCKS

➡ GOLDENEYE
A few nest in Scotland, but mainly a winter visitor from northern Europe. Seen on the sea and inland lakes, often in small flocks. Dives frequently. 46cm.

♀

♂

◀ RED-BREASTED MERGANSER
Breeds by lakes and rivers. Seldom seen inland in winter, but visits many coastal areas and open sea. Dives for fish. 58cm.

♀

♂

➡ GOOSANDER
Most British goosanders nest in the north and west. Likes large lakes in winter. Dives for fish. Look for shaggy crest on female. 66cm.

♀

♂

◀ SHELDUCK
Common around most sandy coasts, especially estuaries. Often in flocks. Groups of young join together in late summer. Looks slow and heavy in flight. 61cm.

Female has no lump on bill

♀

♂

GREBES, HERON, STORK

➡ GREAT CRESTED GREBE

Found on inland waters. Dives for fish. Beautiful courtship displays in spring. May be seen on sea in winter. 48cm.

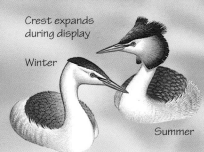

Crest expands during display

Winter

Summer

⬅ LITTLE GREBE OR DABCHICK

Common on inland waters, but secretive and hard to spot. Call is a shrill trill. 27cm.

Winter

Summer

➡ GREY HERON

Usually seen near water. Nests in colonies in trees. Eats fish, frogs and small mammals. 92cm.

Head draws back and legs stick out when flying

⬅ WHITE STORK

Very rare in Britain. Likes wet areas. Will nest on buildings and pylons in Europe. 102cm.

BIRDS OF PREY

➡ OSPREY
Rare summer visitor to Britain. Some nest in Scotland, but seen further south on its migration to Africa. Plunges into water to catch fish. 56cm.

Upper parts are dark brown

Wings narrower than buzzard's

Long broad wings

⬅ GOLDEN EAGLE
Lives in Scottish Highlands. Young birds have white on wings and tail. Glides for long distances. Bigger than buzzard. 83cm.

➡ RED KITE
This rare bird nests in oak woods in mid Wales. Recently released in Scotland and England and increasing in numbers. Soars for long periods. 62cm.

Long forked tail

Notice the pale wing patches

◀ BUZZARD
Large bird of prey with broad wings. Often seen soaring over moors and farmland as it hunts. Rarer in southern and eastern England. 54cm.

Female is larger and browner than male ♀

▶ SPARROWHAWK
Broad-winged hawk. Hunts small birds along hedges and woodland edges. Never hovers. Male 30cm. Female 38cm.

♂

Long pointed wings and tail

♀

♂

◀ KESTREL
Well-known for the way it hovers when hunting, especially alongside motorways. Some nest in towns. Eats birds, insects and small mammals. 34cm.

BIRDS OF PREY

➡ HOBBY
Catches large insects and birds in the air. Summer visitor to southern England. Look on heaths and near water. 33cm.

Tail shorter and wings longer than kestrel

⬅ GOSHAWK
Looks like a large sparrowhawk. Lives in woods. Rare in Britain. Male 48cm. Female 58cm.

➡ PEREGRINE
Lives on sea cliffs or inland crags. Hunts over estuaries and marshes in winter. Dives on flying birds at great speed. 38-48cm.

⬅ HONEY BUZZARD
Summer visitor to British woodlands. Eats mainly grubs of wasps and bees. Rare. 51-59cm.

RAILS, CRAKE

➡ MOORHEN
Lives near ponds, lakes or
streams. Sits high in water
when swimming. Notice
red bill and white tail.
Young are brown. 33cm.

⬅ COOT
A water bird. Dives for
food. Has a white bill and
forehead. Look for its
unusual feet, which have
lobes on long toes. Flocks
in winter. 38cm.

➡ CORNCRAKE
Difficult to see as it
lives in long grass.
Repeats "crex-crex"
cry monotonously,
especially after dark.
Rare in Britain. 27cm.

⬅ WATER RAIL
Secretive bird that lives
in reed beds. Listen for
its piglet-like squeal. Legs
trail in flight. Swims for
short distances. 28cm.

21

GAME BIRDS

➡️ **RED GROUSE**
➡️ **WILLOW GROUSE**

Red grouse lives on
moors in Britain.
Willow grouse lives
in northern Europe.
Willow grouse
is white in
winter. 36cm.

Red
grouse

Willow
grouse

Winter

Summer

In summer, the male's
plumage is browner
and the female's
yellower than in
autumn

Winter

⬅️ **PTARMIGAN**

Lives on barren mountain
tops in the north. Has
three different plumages
and is well camouflaged.
Allows people to get
close. 34cm.

Autumn

➡️ **BLACK GROUSE**

Found on edge of
moorland, sometimes
perched in trees.
Groups of males display
together at an area
known as a "lek".
Male 53cm.
Female 41cm.

♂

♀

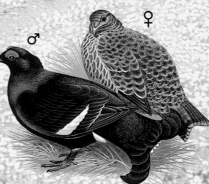

22

➡ CAPERCAILLIE
Lives in pine forests in parts of Scotland. Eats pine shoots. Male 86cm. Female 61cm.

⬅ GREY PARTRIDGE
Often lives in small groups. Likes farmland with hedges. Call is a grating "kirr-ic". Rare in Ireland. 30cm.

➡ PHEASANT
Lives on farmland with hedges. Often reared as game. Roosts in trees. Nests on ground. Male 87cm. Female 58cm.

Look for long tail

Males can vary in colour and often have a white neck ring

⬅ RED-LEGGED PARTRIDGE
Common in southern and eastern Britain. Fields and open sandy areas. Often runs rather than flies. 34cm.

WADERS

White collar in winter

◄ OYSTERCATCHER
Usually seen near the sea, especially in winter. Nests inland in Scotland and parts of England. Feeds on shellfish. 43cm.

Summer

White wing bars show in flight

➤ LAPWING
A farmland bird which flocks in winter. Looks black and white from a distance. Displays in the air in breeding season. Calls "pee-wit". 30cm.

Broad, rounded wings

Summer

◄ TURNSTONE
Likes shingle or rocky shores. Turns stones over to find food. Does not nest in Britain, but can be seen most months. 23cm.

Winter

24

➡ RINGED PLOVER

Usually found near the sea, but sometimes by inland lakes. Likes sandy or shingle shores. Seen all the year round. 19cm.

Summer

Juvenile

Broad white bar on wing

Adult

Notice yellow eye-ring

⬅ LITTLE RINGED PLOVER

Summer visitor. Most common in southeast England. Likes gravel pits and shingle banks inland. Legs are yellowish. 15cm.

Golden plover in winter

Northern Europe

➡ GOLDEN PLOVER

Breeds on upland moors, but found in flocks on coastal marshes or lowland farms in winter. 28cm.

Southern Europe

WADERS

➤ REDSHANK

Breeds on sea shores and wet meadows. Look for white on rump and back edges of wings in flight. 28cm.

Red legs

◄ GREENSHANK

Rarer and slightly bigger than redshank. Seen in spring and autumn on coasts or inland. Some nest in northern Scotland. 30cm.

➤ COMMON SANDPIPER

Summer visitor to upland streams and lakes. Visits wet areas in lowland Britain in spring and autumn. Wags tail and bobs. 20cm.

Summer

Winter

White wing bar

Summer

◄ BLACK-TAILED GODWIT

A few nest in wet meadows in Britain, but more seen on coasts during autumn and winter. 41cm.

➡ BAR-TAILED GODWIT

Smaller than black-tailed godwit. Most are seen in spring and autumn, but some winter on east coast mud flats or estuaries. 37cm.

Winter

Pale rump

No wing bar

⬅ CURLEW

Britain's largest wader. Nests on moors and upland farmland. Seen on coasts at other times of year. Song is "courli". 48-64cm.

Look for stripe on head

Bill shorter than curlew's

➡ WHIMBREL

Like a small curlew. A few nest in heather in northern Scotland. Many more visit Britain's coasts in spring and autumn. 40cm.

WADERS

Winter

Summer

← DUNLIN
A common visitor to
seashores, but nests on
moorland in the north.
Often seen in flocks.
Beak straight or curved
down. 19cm.

Winter

➡ KNOT
Seen in huge flocks in
winter. Likes sand or mud
flats in estuaries. Rare
inland. Mainly a winter
visitor. Breeds in the
Arctic. 25cm.

← SANDERLING
Seen on coasts in winter.
Runs along water's
edge on sandy beaches,
where it catches small
animals washed up by
waves. 20cm.

Winter

Summer

♂

♀

➡ RUFF
Seen in autumn and
spring. A few winter
in wet places, and
some stay to nest. Male
29cm. Female 23cm.

Winter

➡ WOODCOCK
Secretive bird. Lives in damp woodland. Does a bat-like display flight over woods at dusk in early summer. 34cm.

Snipe in flight

Woodcock in flight

⬅ SNIPE
Lives in wet fields, marshes or lake edges. Hard to see on the ground, but rises up with a zig-zag flight when disturbed. 27cm.

➡ AVOCET
Nests on coastal marshes in eastern England. Spends winter in flocks on southern estuaries. Rare inland. 43cm.

29

PIGEONS, DOVES

➡ WOODPIGEON
Largest of the pigeons.
Common on farmland
and in woods and towns.
Forms large flocks. 41cm.

White on
wings

Grey rump.
No white
on wings

⬅ STOCK DOVE
Nests in holes in trees or in
rock faces. Feeds on the
ground, often with
woodpigeons. Sometimes
seen in flocks. 33cm.

➡ ROCK DOVE
➡ TOWN PIGEON
Town pigeons are descended
from rock doves which are
usually found in small groups
on sea cliffs. 33cm.

Town pigeons   White rump

White
on tail

⬅ COLLARED DOVE
Found in parks, large
gardens, or near farm
buildings. Feeds mainly
on grain. 30cm.

➡ TURTLE DOVE
Summer visitor to England
and Wales. Woods, parks
and farmland. Listen
for purring call. 28cm.

White
edge
to tail

AUKS, FULMAR

Neck and throat are white in winter

Summer

◄ RAZORBILL

Look for its flat-sided bill. Nests in colonies on cliffs and rocky shores. Spends winter at sea. Dives for fish. Often seen with guillemots. 41cm.

➡ GUILLEMOT

Nests in large groups on cliffs. Slimmer than a razorbill. Northern birds have white eye-ring and line on heads. 42cm.

Neck and throat are white in winter

Summer

◄ FULMAR

Nests in colonies on ledges on sea cliffs. Often glides close to the waves on stiff wings. Can be seen near cliffs all round our coasts. 47cm.

➡ PUFFIN

Lives on rocky islands and sea cliffs in the north and west of Britain. Nests in burrows in the ground, or between rocks. 30cm.

Colourful beak and reddish feet in summer

GULLS

➡ BLACK-HEADED GULL

Common near the sea and inland. Nests in colonies. Look for a white front edge on its long wings. 37cm.

Winter

Dark brown head in summer only

⬅ LESSER BLACK-BACKED GULL

Mainly a summer visitor to coasts or inland. Some spend winter in Britain. Head streaked with grey in winter. 53cm.

Legs yellow in summer

➡ GREAT BLACK-BACKED GULL

Britain's largest gull. Not very common inland. Nests on rocky coasts. Often solitary. Legs pinkish. 66cm.

⬅ COMMON GULL

Some nest in Scotland and Ireland. Seen further south and often inland in winter. 41cm.

GULL, TERNS

Summer

◄ HERRING GULL
Common in ports and
seaside towns. Scrounges
food from people. Will
nest on buildings. Young's
plumage is mottled brown
for first three years. 56cm.

Arctic tern
in summer

► ARCTIC TERN,
► COMMON TERN
Both species most likely to
be seen near the sea, but
common tern also nests
inland. Both dive into
water to catch fish.
34cm.

Common tern's
bill has black tip

Summer

◄ BLACK TERN
A spring and autumn
visitor. Can be seen flying
low over lakes, dipping
down to pick food
from surface.
24cm.

Summer

Autumn

► LITTLE TERN
A summer visitor.
Nests in small groups
on shingle beaches.
Dives for fish. 24cm.

Yellow bill
with
black tip

Summer

OWLS

➡ BARN OWL
Its call is an eerie shriek.
Often nests in old
buildings or hollow trees.
Hunts small mammals
and roosting birds
at night. 34cm.

*Birds with dark
faces and breasts
are found in north
and east Europe*

*Bouncing
flight*

⬅ LITTLE OWL
Small, flat-headed owl.
Flies low over farmland
and hunts at dusk. Nests
in tree-holes. Bobs up and
down when curious. 22cm.

➡ TAWNY OWL
Calls with familiar "hoot".
Hunts at night where
there are woods or
old trees. Eats small
mammals or birds.
38cm.

⬅ PYGMY OWL
The smallest European
owl. Found in mountain
forests, but not in Britain.
Has a whistling "keeoo"
call. Hunts small birds in
flight. 16cm.

➡ SHORT-EARED OWL

Hunts small mammals in daylight and at dusk. Likes open country. Perches on the ground. Fierce-looking. 37cm.

⬅ LONG-EARED OWL

A secretive night-hunting owl of thick pine woods. Roosts during the day. Long "ear" tufts cannot be seen in flight. 34cm.

➡ TENGMALM'S OWL

Small owl that lives in northern and central European forests. Very rare visitor to Britain. Hunts at night. Nests in tree-holes. 25cm.

⬅ SCOPS OWL

Very rare visitor from southern Europe. Gives monotonous "kiu" call from hidden perch. Hunts only at night. 19cm.

HOOPOE, NIGHTJAR, CUCKOO, KINGFISHER

➡ HOOPOE
Rare visitor to Britain, seen mainly in spring. More common in southern Europe. Probes ground for insects with its long bill. 28cm.

Male has white spots on wings

⬅ NIGHTJAR
Rarely seen in daylight. Listen for churring call at night when it hunts insects. Summer migrant to heathland. 27cm.

➡ CUCKOO
Male's song well known. Female has bubbling call. Found all over Britain in summer. Looks like a sparrowhawk in flight. 30cm.

Juvenile Cuckoo

⬅ KINGFISHER
Small and brilliantly coloured. Seen near lakes and rivers. Dives for fish. Listen for shrill whistle. 17cm.

Usually flies low and straight over water

WOODPECKERS

➡ BLACK WOODPECKER
Size of a rook. Found in forests in Europe, especially old pine woods, except in Britain. Can be confused with crow in flight. 46cm.

Male (shown here) has red crown. Female has red patch on back of head.

Large white patches on wings

➡ LESSER SPOTTED WOODPECKER
Sparrow-sized. Lacks white wing patches of great spotted woodpecker. Male has red crown. Open woodland. Not in Scotland. 14cm.

Yellow-green rump

⬅ GREAT SPOTTED WOODPECKER
Size of a blackbird. Found in woods all over Britain. Drums on trees in spring. 23cm.

Striped back

⬅ GREEN WOODPECKER
Pigeon-sized. Often feeds on ground. Open woods and parks. Quite common in England and Wales. Rare in Scotland. Has a laugh-like call. 32cm.

Woodpeckers do not live in Ireland. They all have bouncing flight

SWIFT, SWALLOW, MARTINS

➡ SWIFT

A common migrant that visits Britain from May to August. Flies fast, often in flocks. Common to town and country. Listen for its screaming call. 17cm.

Swift's tail is forked

Catches insects in flight

Swallow's tail has streamers when adult

⬅ SWALLOW

Summer migrant, seen from April to October. Prefers country, often near water. Nests on rafters or ledges in buldings. 19cm.

➡ HOUSE MARTIN

Summer migrant. Builds cup-shaped nest under eaves. Found in town and country. Catches insects in flight. 13cm.

White rump

White underparts

Brown back

Brown band on breast

⬅ SAND MARTIN

Summer migrant. Groups nest in holes in sandy cliffs and other soft banks. Often seen in flocks, catching insects over water. 12cm.

LARKS, PIPITS, DUNNOCK

White outer tail feathers

Pale back edges to wings

◄ SKYLARK
Lives in open country, especially farmland. Rises to a great height, hovers, and sails down singing. 18cm.

➡ CRESTED LARK
Not often in Britain, but widespread in central and southern Europe. Open, often barren, areas. 17cm.

Orange outer tail feathers

◄ MEADOW PIPIT
Most common on upland moors, but also in fields, marshes and other open areas, especially in winter. 14.5cm.

➡ TREE PIPIT
Summer migrant to heaths and places with scattered trees or bushes. Often perches on branches. 15cm.

◄ DUNNOCK
Common, even in gardens. Feeds under bird tables. Mouse-like walk. Often flicks wings. 14.5cm.

WAGTAILS

➤ **PIED WAGTAIL**
➤ **WHITE WAGTAIL**
Only the pied wagtail is usually seen in Britain. White wagtails are widespread elsewhere in Europe. Common, even in towns. 18cm.

Pied wagtail

Juveniles of both kinds are grey

White wagtail

⬅ **GREY WAGTAIL**
Usually nests near fast-flowing water in hilly areas. Paler yellow in winter, when it visits lowland waters. 18cm.

Male has black throat

Summer ♂

Blue-headed wagtail, central Europe ♂

Yellow wagtail, Britain and Ireland ♂

➤ **BLUE-HEADED WAGTAIL**
➤ **YELLOW WAGTAIL**
Two different forms of the same species. Summer visitor to grassy places near water. Yellow wagtail only seen in Britain. 17cm.

♂

Spanish wagtail, Spain and Portugal

♂

Ashy-headed wagtail, southern Europe

All the birds on this page wag their tails up and down

WAXWING, DIPPER, WREN, SHRIKES

Resembles a starling in flight

← WAXWING
Rare winter visitor from northern Europe. Feeds on berries. May be seen in towns. 17cm.

→ DIPPER
Feeds in fast-flowing hill streams and rivers. Walks underwater to find food. 18cm.

Northern Europe

Britain and central Europe

← WREN
Very small. Found almost everywhere. Loud song finishes with a trill. Never still for long. 9.5cm.

Flies fast and straight on tiny, rounded wings

→ RED-BACKED SHRIKE
Rare visitor to Britain. Catches and eats insects, small birds, etc. 17cm.

Sticks food on thorns to store it

♂ ♀

← GREAT GREY SHRIKE
Winter visitor to open country in Britain. Feeds on birds and mammals. Often hovers. 24cm.

WARBLERS

➡ SEDGE WARBLER
Summer migrant. Nests in thick vegetation, usually near water, but also in drier areas. Sings from cover and is often difficult to see. 13cm.

White stripe over eye

Reddish-brown rump

⬅ REED WARBLER
Summer visitor. Nests in reed beds or among waterside plants, mainly in the south of England. Hard to spot. Look for it flitting over reeds. 13cm.

Brown above, paler below

➡ GARDEN WARBLER
Summer visitor. Sings from dense cover and is hard to see. Likes undergrowth or thick hedges. Song can be confused with blackcap's. 14cm.

♂

Female's cap is reddish-brown

♀

⬅ BLACKCAP
Common summer visitor to woods or places with trees. Always moving from perch to perch as it sings. 14cm.

Male has grey head and white throat. Females and young have brown heads

♂

← WHITETHROAT

A summer migrant, which hides itself in thick, low bushes. Sometimes sings its fast, scratchy song in flight. Flight is short and jerky. 14cm.

➡ WILLOW WARBLER

Summer migrant. Commonest British warbler. Its song, which comes down the scale, is the best way of telling it from the chiffchaff. 11cm.

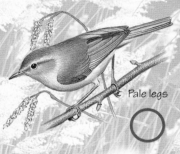

Pale legs

Dark legs

← CHIFFCHAFF

Summer migrant, often arriving in March. A few spend the winter in Britain. Its repetitive "chiff-chaff" song can be heard in woods and from bushes. 11cm.

➡ WOOD WARBLER

Summer migrant to open woods. Sings from a branch, repeating a note faster and faster until it becomes a trill. 13cm.

Yellow breast, white underparts

FLYCATCHERS, CHATS

♂ ♀

← PIED FLYCATCHER
Catches insects in air. Also feeds on the ground. Summer migrant to old woodland. 13cm.

♂

♀

➡ WHINCHAT
Summer migrant, found in open country. "Tic-tic" call. Perches on tops of bushes and posts. 13cm.

Flicks wings and tail

♀

♂

Colour is duller in winter

← STONECHAT
"Tac-tac" call sounds like stones being knocked together. Found on heaths with gorse, especially near the sea. 13cm.

♂ ♀

➡ WHEATEAR
Summer migrant to moors and barren areas, but also seen elsewhere in the spring and autumn. 15cm.

White rump and black tail

➡ SPOTTED FLYCATCHER

Summer migrant. Likes open woods, parks and country gardens. Catches insects in flight. 14cm.

Sits upright, often on a bare branch

♀

♂

➡ BLACK REDSTART

A few nest on buildings or on cliffs in Britain. Some spend winter in south of England. Flicks its tail. 14cm.

Male and female look alike

⬅ REDSTART

A summer migrant to open woods, heaths and parks. Constantly flicks its tail. 14cm.

♀

♂

⬅ ROBIN

Woodland bird that is familiar in gardens. Sings in winter and spring. "Tic-tic" is its call of alarm. 14cm.

Reddish tail

➡ NIGHTINGALE

Secretive summer migrant. Best found by listening for its song in May and June. 17cm.

THRUSHES, ORIOLE

➡ FIELDFARE
Winter visitor, but a few
nest in England and
Scotland. Flocks can be
seen in autumn, eating
berries. 25.5cm.

⬅ RING OUZEL
Summer migrant to moors
and mountains. Visits
lower areas on migration.
Shyer than blackbird.
Loud piping call. 24cm.

*Young are lighter and
spottier than
female*
♀

➡ BLACKBIRD
Lives where there are
trees and bushes, often
in parks and gardens.
Loud musical song.
Clucking alarm call. 25cm.

⬅ GOLDEN ORIOLE
Rare summer migrant
most often seen in woods
of eastern England. Hard
to see as it spends a lot of
time in tree-tops. 24cm.

THRUSHES, STARLING

White stripe over eye

◀ REDWING
Winter migrant, but a few nest in Scotland. Feeds on berries in hedges and hunts worms. 21cm.

➡ SONG THRUSH
Found near or in trees or bushes. Well-known for the way it breaks open snail shells. Often in gardens. 23cm.

Smaller than mistle thrush

White under wing

◀ MISTLE THRUSH
Large thrush found in most parts of Britain. Seen on the ground in fields and on moors. 27cm.

White outer tail feathers

Juvenile

Adult in winter

➡ STARLING
A familiar garden bird. Often roosts in huge flocks. Mimics songs of other birds. 22cm.

TITS

➡ LONG-TAILED TIT
Hedgerows and the edges of woods are good places to see groups of these tiny birds. 14cm.

Northern and eastern Europe

Britain and western Europe

⬅ CRESTED TIT
Widespread in Europe, but in Britain only found in a few Scottish pine woods, especially in the Spey Valley. 11cm.

➡ COAL TIT
Likes conifer woods, but often seen in deciduous trees. Large white patch on back of head. 11cm.

⬅ BLUE TIT
Seen in woods and gardens. Often raises its blue cap to form a small crest. Young are less colourful. 11cm.

➡ MARSH TIT
➡ WILLOW TIT
Two birds of deciduous woods. Also visit gardens. 11cm.

Marsh tit has plain wings

TIT, NUTHATCH, CRESTS, TREECREEPER

➡ GREAT TIT
Largest tit. Lives in woodlands and gardens. Nests in holes in trees or will use nestboxes. 14cm.

Broad black band on breast

○

⬅ NUTHATCH
Lives in deciduous woods in England and Wales. Climbs up and down trees in a series of short hops. Very short tail. 14cm.

○

➡ TREECREEPER
Usually seen in woods, climbing up tree trunks and flying down again to search for food. Listen for high-pitched call. 13cm.

○

Firecrest   White stripe over eye

Goldcrest

⬅ FIRECREST
⬅ GOLDCREST
Smallest European birds. Goldcrests are found in woods, especially of pine, all over Britain. Firecrests are much rarer. 9cm.

○

FINCHES

➡ CHAFFINCH
Found in gardens and wherever there are trees and bushes. During winter, often seen in flocks on farmland. 15cm.

♀

♀

Male's head is brown in winter

♂

⬅ BRAMBLING
Winter migrant from northern Europe. Flocks feed on grain and seeds. Likes fruit from beech trees. 15cm.

➡ GREENFINCH
A frequent visitor to gardens, especially in winter. Likely to nest wherever there are trees and bushes. 15cm.

♀

♂

♀

♂

⬅ SISKIN
A small finch which nests in conifers. It sometimes visits gardens in winter to feed on peanuts. 11cm.

♀

♂

White rump
shows in flight

➡ BULLFINCH
Secretive bird often found on edges of woods, and in hedges or gardens. Eats seeds and also buds from fruit trees. 15cm.

♂   ♀

➡ LINNET
Lives on heathland and farmland, but also found in towns, where it may visit gardens. Feeds on the seeds of weeds. Flocks in winter. 13cm.

Lesser
Redpoll

⬅ LESSER REDPOLL
⬅ MEALY REDPOLL
The lesser redpoll is common in birch woods and forestry plantations in Britain. The mealy redpoll lives in northern Europe. 12cm.

Mealy
Redpoll

➡ GOLDFINCH
Feeds on thistle seeds and other weed seeds in open places. Nests in trees. 12cm.

Yellow
wing
bar

CROSSBILL, CROWS

♀ ♂

← CROSSBILL
Nests in pine woods. A slightly different species nests in Scotland. Eats pine seeds. 16cm.

Crossbills are sparrow-sized, with large heads and bills

➡ JAY
Secretive woodland bird. Will visit gardens. Listen for harsh screeching call. Look for white rump in flight. 32cm.

← RAVEN
This large crow lives in wild rocky areas or on rocky coasts. Look for its wedge-shaped tail and huge bill. Croaks. 64cm.

➡ JACKDAW
Small member of the crow family. Found where there are old trees, old buildings, or cliffs. Nests in colonies. Often seen with rooks. 33cm.

← CARRION CROW
← HOODED CROW
Carrion crows more often
seen alone or in pairs.
Hooded crows form
flocks. Carrion is more
widespread than
hooded. 47cm.

Carrion crow - England, Wales
and southern Scotland

Hooded crow - northern
Scotland and Ireland

→ ROOK
Nests in "rookeries" in tops
of trees. Is usually seen in
flocks on farmland. Young
lack bare skin round
beak. Call is
harsh "kaw".
46cm.

Baggy thigh
feathers

← MAGPIE
Seen in both town and
country. Eats many eggs
and young birds in spring.
Long tail is very noticeable
in flight. 46cm.

SPARROWS, BUNTINGS

➡ HOUSE SPARROW
Very common bird. Easy to spot, since it lives near houses and even in busy city centres. Often seen in flocks. 15cm.

♂   ♀

Brown cap and smudge below eye

Male and female look alike

⬅ TREE SPARROW
Usually nests in holes in trees or cliffs. Much less common than house sparrow. 14cm.

♂   ♀

➡ YELLOWHAMMER
Found in open country, especially farmland. Feeds on ground. Forms flocks in winter. Sings from the tops of bushes. 17cm.

♀

⬅ REED BUNTING
Most common near water, but some nest in dry areas with long grass. May visit bird tables in winter. 15cm.

♀

♂

➡ CORN BUNTING
Nests in cornfields. Sings from posts, bushes or overhead wires. 18cm.

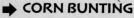

FEEDING BIRDS

You can encourage birds to visit a windowsill or garden by putting out food. The best time to feed birds is in the winter when natural food is in short supply. In the spring only put out wild bird seed (from a pet shop) as baby birds need mainly foods such as grubs and insects.

Blue tit feeding on peanuts

WHAT TO FEED BIRDS

Cheese, fat, nuts, dried fruit and baked potatoes (cut in half) are good high-energy foods for birds. Raw, unsalted peanuts are popular. You can also buy wild bird seed from pet shops. Remember to clear and clean bird tables and bird-feeders at regular intervals.

WATER

If you put out food, you should also provide water for drinking and bathing. A large dish, or an old dustbin lid on bricks makes a simple bird bath. Don't forget to break the ice in cold weather and clean the bath regularly.

MAKE A BIRD CAKE

You can make a bird cake from seeds, nuts, oatmeal and dried fruit. Put 500g of the mixture in a heat-resistant bowl. Melt 250g of solid fat in a saucepan over a low heat. Carefully pour the fat over the mixture and leave to set.

Turn the cake out when it is cold. Put it on a bird table or feeding station whole.

MAKE A BIRD-FEEDER

To make a simple bird-feeder you need two clean,
empty cartons, a pencil, some scissors,
a stapler and some garden wire.

1. Use the stapler to
close up the top of one
carton. Draw and cut
along the dotted lines
shown here.

2. Cut two sides from
the other carton,
leaving them joined.
Use scissors to score a
line 1cm each side of
the join. Fold along
these lines to make
the roof.

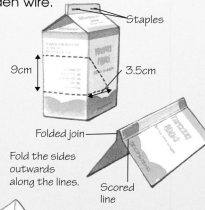

Staples

9cm

3.5cm

Folded join

Fold the sides
outwards
along the lines.

Scored
line

Drainage holes

Wire

Staple

Roof

Overhang

Pencil

3. Make two drainage
holes in the base. Then
staple on the roof,
making sure it overhangs
the holes. Push the pencil
through the feeder to
make a perch.

4. Use the wire to hang
the feeder from a bird
table or tree. If you don't
have a garden, hang the
feeder from a bracket
fixed to an outside window
frame, but get permission
to attach the bracket first.

USEFUL WORDS

This list explains some of the terms used in this book. Words in *italics* are defined separately.

bar – a natural mark across a feather or group of feathers.

belly – part of a bird's body between its *breast* and tail.

bill – another word for beak.

bird of prey – a bird such as an eagle which hunts other animals for food.

breast – part of a bird's body between its throat and *belly*.

breeding season – the time of year when a pair of birds build a nest, mate, lay eggs and look after their young. In Britain this is usually spring.

colony – a group of birds of the same species nesting close together.

conifers – trees such as pines and firs that have cones, and needle-shaped leaves.

courtship display – when a male bird attracts a mate. Some birds show off their *plumage*; others do a display in the air.

cover – anywhere that birds hide themselves - hedges, bushes, thick grass, etc.

crown – the top part of a bird's head.

flock – a group of birds of the same *species* feeding or travelling together

game bird – a bird such as a pheasant or partridge that is hunted by humans for food.

habitat – the place where a *species* of bird lives.

hover – to stay in one place in the air, flapping the wings fast.

juvenile – a young bird that does not yet have full, adult *plumage*.

lek – an area where the male birds of some *species* gather to perform a *courtship display* to females.

migration – a regular movement of birds from one place to another. For example, many birds migrate from the breeding area to a warmer place, where they spend the winter.

moult – to lose old feathers and grow new ones. All birds do this at least once a year.

nape – the back of a bird's neck.

perch – to stand on a branch, etc. by gripping with the toes; or the place where a bird perches.

plumage – a bird's feathers.

primaries – the large, outer wing feathers.

roost – to go to sleep (when describing a bird only). Alternatively, a place where birds sleep.

rump – the area of a bird's body above its tail.

secondaries – the inner wing feathers.

species – a group of birds that all look alike and behave in the same way, e.g. herring gull is the name of one species.

wader – one of a group of long-legged birds that live near water and often wade in search of food.

GOING FURTHER

If you have access to the Internet, you can visit these Web sites to find out more about birds and birdwatching. For links to these sites, go to the Usborne Quicklinks Web site at **www.usborne-quicklinks.com** and enter the keyword "spotters".

Internet safety

When using the Internet, please follow the **Internet safety guidelines** shown on the Usborne Quicklinks Web site.

WEB SITE 1 The Web site of the RSPB, the Royal Society for the Protection of Birds (see opposite page for more information).

WEB SITE 2 A young, friendly Web site with information on different bird species, bird anatomy, bird facts, and lots of things to make and do.

WEB SITE 3 Find out how to attract and care for wild birds that visit your garden.

WEB SITE 4 Species profiles, a photo gallery and a reference section with information on bird care.

WEB SITE 5 Detailed information about how birds fly.

WEB SITE 6 Owls of the world with sound clips of their calls.

WEB SITE 7 Everything you need to know about the wildlife of wetlands.

WEB SITE 8 Listen to bird songs and find out how to make recordings.

WEB SITE 9 Information for UK birdwatchers with news of rare sightings and tips for identifying birds.

Usborne Publishing is not responsible and does not accept liability for the availability or content of any Web site other than its own, or for any exposure to harmful, offensive, or inaccurate material which may appear on the Web.

WEB SITE 10 The Worldwide Fund for Nature. (You can search this site for information about birds.)

WEB SITE 11 Tips and ideas to help you have fun watching birds.

WEB SITE 12 Links to Web sites all over the world where you can see nesting birds via Web cams.

WEB SITE 13 - RSPB Youth section.

JOIN THE RSPB WILDLIFE EXPLORERS

If you want to find out more about birds and other wildlife, become a member of the RSPB Wildlife Explorers, the junior section of the RSPB (the Royal Society for the Protection of Birds). Joining the RSPB Wildlife Explorers will give you the chance to take part in projects and competitions and meet other people who share your interest. This is what you will get when you join:

- Your own membership card.
- Free entry to more than 120 RSPB nature reserves.
- *Bird Life* magazine packed with photos, articles and things to do and make, six times a year.
- The chance to join activity days, holidays and local groups.

Find out more by writing to: RSPB Wildlife Explorers, The Lodge, Sandy, Bedfordshire SG19 2DL, or telephone: 01767 680551, or go to Usborne Quicklinks at **www.usborne-quicklinks.com** and click on **Web site 13** for a link to the RSPB Youth Web site.

SCORECARD

The birds on this score-card are in alphabetical order. Fill in the date on which you spot a bird beside its name. A common bird scores 5 points, and a rare one is worth 25. After a day's spotting, add up the points you have scored on a sheet of paper and keep a record of them. See if you can score more points another day.

Species (Name of bird)	Score	Date spotted	Species (Name of bird)	Score	Date spotted
Arctic tern	15		Brambling	15	
Avocet	20		Brent goose	20	
Barnacle goose	20		Bullfinch	15	
Barn owl	15		Buzzard	15	
Bar-tailed godwit	20		Canada goose	5	
Bean goose	25		Capercaillie	25	
Bewick's swan	20		Carrion crow	5	
Blackbird	5		Chaffinch	5	
Blackcap	15		Chiffchaff	10	
Black grouse	20		Coal tit	10	
Black-headed gull	5		Collared dove	5	
Black redstart	20		Common gull	15	
Black-tailed godwit	20		Common sandpiper	15	
Black tern	20		Common tern	15	
Black woodpecker	25		Coot	10	
Blue-headed wagtail	25		Cormorant	10	
Blue tit	5		Corn bunting	15	

Species (Name of bird)	Score	Date spotted	Species (Name of bird)	Score	Date spotted
Corncrake	25		Great grey shrike	25	
Crested lark	25		Great spotted woodpecker	10	
Crested tit	20		Great tit	5	
Crossbill	20		Greenfinch	10	
Cuckoo	10		Greenshank	20	
Curlew	15		Green woodpecker	15	
Dipper	15		Grey heron	10	
Dunlin	10		Greylag goose	10	
Dunnock	5		Grey partridge	15	
Eider	15		Grey wagtail	15	
Fieldfare	10		Guillemot	15	
Firecrest	25		Herring gull	5	
Fulmar	10		Hobby	20	
Gannet	15		Honey buzzard	25	
Garden warbler	15		Hooded crow	10	
Goldcrest	10		Hoopoe	25	
Golden eagle	25		House martin	10	
Goldeneye	15		House sparrow	5	
Golden oriole	25		Jackdaw	10	
Golden plover	15		Jay	10	
Goldfinch	10		Kestrel	10	
Goosander	20		Kingfisher	15	
Goshawk	25		Knot	15	
Great black-backed gull	15		Lapwing	10	
Great crested grebe	10		Lesser black-backed gull	10	

Species (Name of bird)	Score	Date spotted	Species (Name of bird)	Score	Date spotted
Lesser redpoll	15		Pied wagtail	10	
Lesser spotted woodpecker	20		Pink-footed goose	20	
Linnet	10		Pintail	20	
Little grebe	15		Pochard	15	
Little owl	15		Ptarmigan	20	
Little ringed plover	20		Puffin	20	
Little tern	20		Pygmy owl	25	
Long-eared owl	20		Raven	15	
Long-tailed tit	10		Razorbill	15	
Magpie	5		Red-backed shrike	25	
Mallard	5		Red-breasted merganser	20	
Marsh tit	15		Red grouse	15	
Meadow pipit	10		Red kite	20	
Mealy redpoll	25		Red-legged partridge	10	
Mistle thrush	10		Redshank	10	
Moorhen	5		Redstart	15	
Mute swan	10		Redwing	10	
Nightingale	15		Reed bunting	15	
Nightjar	15		Reed warbler	15	
Nuthatch	15		Ringed plover	15	
Osprey	20		Ring ouzel	15	
Oystercatcher	15		Robin	5	
Peregrine	20		Rock dove	25	
Pheasant	5		Rook	10	
Pied flycatcher	20		Ruff	20	

Species (Name of bird)	Score	Date spotted	Species (Name of bird)	Score	Date spotted
Sanderling	15		Tree sparrow	20	
Sand martin	15		Tufted duck	10	
Scops owl	25		Turnstone	15	
Sedge warbler	15		Turtle dove	15	
Shag	15		Water rail	15	
Shelduck	15		Waxwing	20	
Short-eared owl	20		Wheatear	15	
Shoveler	15		Whimbrel	20	
Siskin	15		Whinchat	15	
Skylark	10		White-fronted goose	20	
Snipe	15		White stork	25	
Song thrush	10		Whitethroat	15	
Sparrowhawk	10		White wagtail	25	
Spotted flycatcher	10		Whooper swan	20	
Starling	5		Wigeon	15	
Stock dove	15		Willow grouse	25	
Stonechat	15		Willow warbler	10	
Swallow	10		Woodcock	20	
Swift	10		Woodpigeon	5	
Tawny owl	15		Wood warbler	20	
Teal	15		Wren	5	
Tengmalm's owl	25		Yellowhammer	10	
Town pigeon	5		Yellow wagtail	15	
Treecreeper	15				
Tree pipit	15				

INDEX

PART TWO
FLOWERS

Part Two – Flowers
Written by Christopher J. Humphries, Department of Botany, The Natural History
Museum, London, England
Illustrated by Hilary Burn
Consultant: Richard Scott
Edited by Rosie Dickins, Jessica Datta and Sue Jacquemier
Designed by Nicola Butler
Additional illustrations by Victoria Goaman, Ian Jackson and Michelle Ross

Picture acknowledgements, backgrounds – pages 65, 68-69, 74-119,
122-126 © Digital Vision; pages 66-67, 70-71 © Tony Stone Images;
pages 72-73 © Landlife; pages 120-121 © CORBIS.

CONTENTS

HOW TO USE THIS BOOK

This part of the book is an identification guide to some of the wild flowers of Europe. Take it with you when you go out spotting.

The flowers are arranged by colour to make it easy for you to look them up. This Rosebay Willowherb, for example, appears in the section of the book that shows pink flowers. The picture in the circle below shows a close-up of a Rosebay Willowherb seed, to help you identify the plant. Sometimes there are close-ups of flowers or fruits, too.

Top of plant

Rosebay Willowherb

The height of a plant is measured from its top to ground level

Seed of Rosebay Willowherb (seeds can be seen after the plant has finished flowering)

Ground level

HOW FLOWERS ARE DESCRIBED

Each flower in this book has a picture and a description to help you to identify it. The example here shows you how the descriptions work.

Name and description of flower

➡ **SCARLET PIMPERNEL**

Grows along the ground. Flowers close in bad weather. Black dots under the pointed, oval leaves. Cultivated land. 15cm tall. June-Aug.

Average height of plant

When to see plant in flower

Picture of flower (not drawn to scale)

Flowers may also be blue

Close-up of flower with additional information to help identify plant

Where to find flower

Circle to tick when you spot this flower

AREAS COVERED BY THIS BOOK

The green area on this map shows the countries which are covered by this book. Not all the flowers that grow in these areas appear in the book, and some flowers are more common in one country than another.

British Isles

Mainland Europe

WHAT TO TAKE

When you go out to spot flowers, take the following items with you:

- this book;

- a notepad and a pencil, so that you can record your finds;

- a tape measure, to measure plants;

- a magnifying glass, so you can examine individual flowers and any insects you may find;

- a camera (if you have one), to photograph flowers (see page 121).

Draw the flowers you spot, and note down when and where you found them. Write down the height of the plant, and the colour and shape of the flower heads and leaves. If you see a flower that is not in this book, your notes will help you to identify it from other books later. Don't pick wild flowers – see page 119 for more about protecting them.

SCORECARD

The scorecard at the end of this book gives you a score for each flower you spot. A common flower scores 5 points, and a very rare one is worth 25 points. If you like, you can add up your score after a day out spotting. Some flowers may not be common where you live. Try to spot them if you go on holiday. Other flowers are rare in the wild.

Species (Name of flower)	Score	Date spotted
Daisy	5	20/07/01
Dandelion	5	
Deptford Pink	25	26/06/01
Devil's Bit Scabious	10	17/07/01

Fill in the scorecard like this.

Count rare flowers if you see them in a garden or on television.

ABOUT FLOWERS

These pictures show some different kinds of flowers, and explain some of the words that appear in the book. When you are examining a plant, look closely at the flowerhead to help you to identify it.

Some flowers have petals of even length and lots of stamens.

Buttercup

Petal

All the petals together are called the corolla

Stamens

Bud

Some flowerheads are made up of clusters of tiny flowers.

Daisy

Centre and outside ring are made of lots of tiny flowers.

Some flowers have petals which form hoods and lips.

Common Spotted Orchid

Hood

Lip (insects land here)

The petals of some flowers are joined together.

Foxglove

Bract

Sepal

Corolla

Toadflax

The petals of some flowers form a tube called a spur.

Spur (contains nectar which is drunk by bees)

SHAPES TO LOOK FOR

These pictures show some of the different ways that plants grow. If you look out for these shapes, it will help you to recognize different plants.

An "erect" plant grows straight up from the ground. "Runners" are stems that grow sideways along the ground, as though they are creeping. Some plants grow in thick mats or carpets close to the ground. These are called "mat-forming" plants.

An erect plant

Early
Purple
Orchid

A mat-forming plant

Stonecrop

A plant with runners

Runner

Creeping
Buttercup

FLOWERS, FRUITS AND SEEDS

This is what the inside of a Buttercup looks like. The stigma, style and ovary together form the female part of the flower, or "carpel". The stamens are the male parts. Pollen from the stamens is received by the stigma (this is called pollination). It causes seeds to grow inside the ovary.

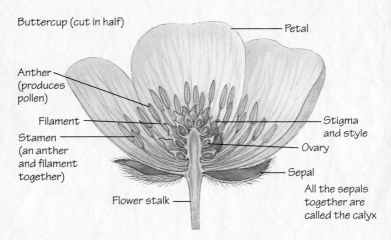

Buttercup (cut in half)

Petal

Anther (produces pollen)

Filament

Stamen (an anther and filament together)

Stigma and style

Ovary

Sepal

All the sepals together are called the calyx

Flower stalk

Some flowers can pollinate themselves and some are pollinated by wind. Other flowers need insects to spread their pollen. These flowers have special scents and markings to attract insects.

The scent and colour of this Meadow Clary flower have attracted a bee

Pollen brushes onto the bee. When bee visits another flower, the stigma will pick up this pollen from its body

FROM FLOWER TO FRUIT

A flower helps a plant to produce seeds. Once a flower is pollinated, the seeds start to develop and the petals wither and fall off. The rest of the flower becomes a fruit containing seeds.

A bee pollinates the Poppy flower

The petals and stamens die

The ovary swells and develops into a fruit

FRUITS AND SEEDS

The seeds of a plant are usually surrounded by a fruit. Different plants have different-looking fruits, so you can recognize plants by their fruits. Here are two examples.

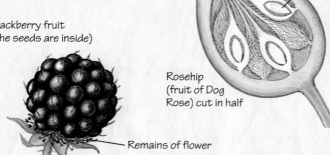

Blackberry fruit (the seeds are inside)

Remains of flower

Seed

Rosehip (fruit of Dog Rose) cut in half

Remains of flower

LEAVES

Even if a plant is not in flower, you can recognize it from its leaves. There are many different leaf shapes.

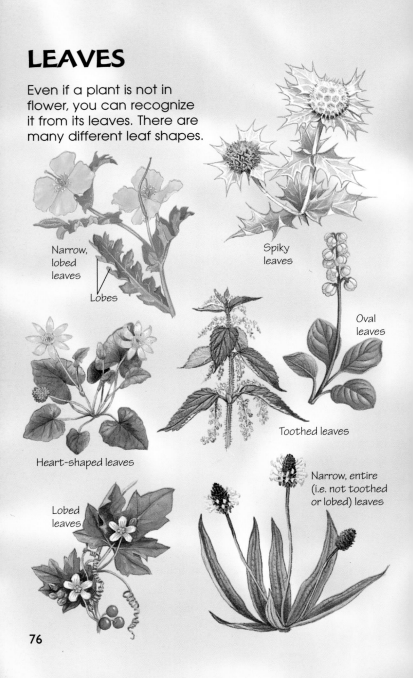

Narrow, lobed leaves

Lobes

Spiky leaves

Oval leaves

Heart-shaped leaves

Toothed leaves

Lobed leaves

Narrow, entire (i.e. not toothed or lobed) leaves

Leaves can also be
arranged in different
ways on the stem
of a plant.

Leaves growing
in whorls around
the stem

Leaves growing
in a rosette
around the base
of the stem

Leaves growing
alternately on
the stem

Leaves
growing in
opposite
pairs on
the stem

Leaves
growing in a
spiral around
the stem

77

YELLOW FLOWERS

Look for these flowers in damp places, such as ditches, marshes and water meadows.

➡ LESSER CELANDINE
A small, creeping plant with glossy, heart-shaped leaves. Shiny yellow flowers. Look in damp, shady woods and waysides. 7cm tall. March-May.

Each flower has four yellow sepals

◀ ALTERNATE-LEAVED GOLDEN SAXIFRAGE
Small plant with round, toothed leaves and greenish-yellow flowers. Look in wet places. 7cm tall. April-July.

➡ CREEPING BUTTERCUP
Look for the long runners near the ground. Hairy, deeply-divided leaves. Shiny yellow flowers. Common weed of grassy places. May-Aug.

Runner

➡ CREEPING JENNY

A creeping, mat-forming plant with shiny, oval leaves. Yellow flowers are 1.5-2.5cm across. In grassy places and under hedges. June-Aug.

Opposite leaves

➡ COWSLIP

Easily recognized in April and May by the single clusters of nodding flowers. Rosette of leaves at base. Grows in meadows. 15cm tall.

Sepals

Close-up of flower

⬅ COMMON MEADOW RUE

Tall, erect plant with dense clusters of flowers. Leaves have 3-4 lobes. Look in marshy fields and fens. Up to 80cm tall. July-Aug.

YELLOW FLOWERS

Look for these flowers
in woods, hedgerows
and heaths.

Cluster of fruits

➡ HERB BENNET
or WOOD AVENS
Fruits have hooks which
catch on clothes and
animals' fur. Woods,
hedges and shady
places. Up to 50cm tall.
June-Aug.

⬅ YELLOW PIMPERNEL
Like Creeping Jenny,
but smaller, with more
pointed leaves. Slender,
trailing stems. The flowers
close in dull weather.
Woods and hedges.
May-Sept.

Barberries can be
used to make jam

➡ BARBERRY
A shrub with spiny
branches. Bees visit the
drooping flowers. Look
for the red berries. Hedges
and scrubland. Up to
100cm tall. May-June.

Close-up
of flower

➡ YELLOW ARCHANGEL

Also called Weasel Snout.
Look for the red-brown
markings on the yellow
petals. Opposite pairs of
leaves. Common in woods.
40cm tall. May-June.

⬅ WOOD GROUNDSEL

Erect plant growing on
heaths and sandy soil.
The petals of the small
flowers curl back.
Narrow lobed leaves.
60cm tall. July-Sept.

Whorl of
flowers

⬅ PRIMROSE

Well-known spring
flower, with hairy stems
and rosette of large
leaves. Often grows in
patches. Woods,
hedges and fields.
15cm tall. Dec.-May.

81

YELLOW FLOWERS

Look for these flowers in open, grassy places, such as heaths and commons.

✒ FURZE or GORSE
Also called Whin. Dark green, spiny bush on heaths and commons. The bright yellow flowers smell like almonds. 100-200cm tall. March-June.

Close-up of flower

➡ BIRD'S FOOT TREFOIL
Also called Bacon and Eggs because the yellow flowers are streaked with red. Look for this small, creeping plant on grassy banks and downs. May-June.

The seed pods look like birds' claws

Seeds

Silverweed

Creeping Cinquefoil

⬅ SILVERWEED
⬅ CREEPING CINQUEFOIL
Both spread close to the ground with long, rooting runners. Hedge banks and grassy places. May-Aug.

← COMMON ST. JOHN'S WORT

Look for see-through dots on the narrow, oval leaves, and black dots on the petals and sepals. Damp, grassy places. 60cm tall. June-Sept.

→ WOAD

Look for the hanging pods on this tall, erect plant. The leaves were once boiled to make a blue dye. Waysides and dry places. 70cm tall. June-Sept.

Seed pod

Dandelion "clock"

← DANDELION

Common weed with rosette of toothed leaves. The flowers close at night. Look for the "clock" of downy white fruits. Waysides. 15cm tall. March-June.

Close-up of fruit

83

YELLOW FLOWERS

➡ STONECROP
Also called Wallpepper.
Mat-forming plant with
star-shaped flowers.
The thick, fleshy leaves
have a peppery taste.
Dunes, shingle and
walls. June-July.

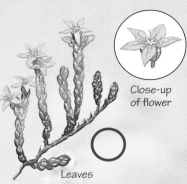

Close-up
of flower

Leaves

⬅ PURSLANE
A low, spreading plant
with red stems. The fleshy,
oval-shaped leaves are
in opposite pairs. A weed
of fields and waste ground.
May-Oct.

Close-up
of flower

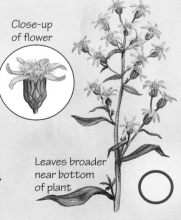

➡ GOLDEN ROD
Erect plant with flowers
on thin spikes. Leaves are
narrower and more
pointed near top of plant.
Woods, banks and cliffs.
40cm tall. July-Sept.

Leaves broader
near bottom
of plant

Close-up of seed pod

◀ RAPE
Common on roadsides. Also grown as a crop, to produce rape-seed oil. Dark blue-green leaves. Flowers grow in clusters and have four petals. Look for the long seed pods. Up to 100cm tall. May-July.

➡ CYPRESS SPURGE
Erect plant with many pale, needle-like leaves. Spray of yellowish flowers. Roadsides and grassy places. Rare in Britain. 40cm tall. May-Aug.

A yellow Wild Pansy

◀ WILD PANSY or HEARTSEASE
The flowers can be violet, yellow, or a mixture of both, or sometimes pink and white. Grassy places and cornfields. 15cm tall. April-Oct.

BLUE FLOWERS

◄ CORNFLOWER

Also called Bluebottle.
Erect plant with greyish,
downy leaves and a
blue flower head.
Cornfields and waste
places. 40cm tall.
July-Aug. Rare.

Seed
pod

Spur

➤ LARKSPUR

Slender plant with
divided, feathery leaves.
The flowers have a long
spur. Cultivated land.
50cm tall. June-July.

Bud

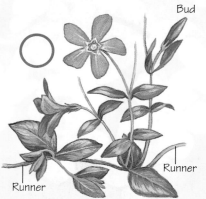

◄ LESSER PERIWINKLE

Creeps along the
ground with long
runners, making leafy
carpets. Shiny, oval
leaves. Woods and
hedges. Flower stems up
to 15cm tall. Feb.-May.

Runner

Runner

➡ VIPER'S BUGLOSS

Long, narrow leaves on rough, hairy stems. Erect or creeping. Pink buds become blue flowers. Waysides and sand dunes. 30cm tall. June-Sept.

Bud

Stamens

Sharp hairs on stem

Flowers have yellow centres

Rosette of leaves

◀ COMMON FORGET-ME-NOT

The curled stems of this hairy plant slowly straighten when it flowers. Flowers turn from pink to blue. Open places. 20cm tall. April-Oct.

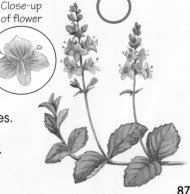

Close-up of flower

➡ COMMON SPEEDWELL

A hairy plant which forms large mats. Pinkish-blue flowers on erect spikes. Opposite, oval leaves. Grassy places and woods. 30cm tall. May-Aug.

87

BLUE FLOWERS

Look for these flowers in damp places.

Flower is shaped like a monk's hood

► COMMON MONKSHOOD

Also called Wolfsbane. Upright plant with spike of flowers at end of stem. Notice hood on flowers and the deeply-divided leaves. Near streams and in damp woods. 70cm tall. June-Sept.

► BROOKLIME

Creeping plant with erect, reddish stems. Shiny, oval leaves in opposite pairs. Used to be eaten in salads. Wet places. 30cm tall. May-Sept.

Close-up of bugle-shaped flower

◄ BUGLE

Creeping plant with erect flower spikes. Glossy leaves in opposite pairs. Stem is square and hairy on two sides. Leaves and stem are purplish. Forms carpets in damp woods. 20cm tall. May-June.

➡ SEA HOLLY

A stiff, spiny plant with grey-blue leaves and round flower heads. Look for it on sandy and shingle beaches. 50cm tall. July-Aug.

Fruiting head

Flower

Flowers grow in whorls

⬅ MEADOW CLARY or MEADOW SAGE

Hairy stem with wrinkled leaves mostly at the base of the plant. Grassy places. 40cm tall. June-July.

➡ BLUEBELL

Also called Wild Hyacinth. Narrow, shiny leaves and clusters of nodding blue flowers. Forms thick carpets in woods. 30cm tall. April-May.

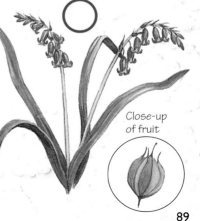

Close-up of fruit

PINK FLOWERS

Look for these flowers in woods or hedges.

➡ WOOD SORREL
A creeping, woodland plant with slender stems and rounded leaves. The white flowers have purplish veins. Woods and hedges. 10cm tall. April-May.

◀ RED HELLEBORINE
Upright plant with pointed leaves and a fleshy stem. Rare plant, protected by law. Woods and shady places. Up to 40cm tall. May-June.

➡ BLACKBERRY or BRAMBLE
Dense, woody plant that climbs up hedges. Sharp prickles on stems and under leaves. Berries are ripe and good to eat in autumn. June-Sept.

Ripe berry

◀ BISTORT

Also called Snakeweed.
Forms patches. Leaves
are narrow. Flowers in
spikes. In meadows,
often near water.
40cm tall. June-Oct.

➡ GREATER BINDWEED

Look for the large, pink
or white, funnel-shaped
flowers. Climbs walls and
hedges in waste places.
Leaves are shaped like
arrowheads. 300cm high.
July-Sept.

Bud

Rose hip
(fruit)

◀ DOG ROSE

Scrambling creeper,
up to 300cm tall,
with thorny stems.
Look for the red fruits,
called rose hips, in
autumn. Hedges and
woods. June-July.

PINK FLOWERS

➡ KNOTGRASS

A weed that spreads
in a thick mat or
grows erect. Waste
ground, fields and
seashores. Stems
can be 100cm long.
July-Oct.

*Close-up
of flower*

Bud

⬅ SOAPWORT

Erect plant with clusters of
scented flowers. The
broad, oval leaves were
once used to make soap.
Near rivers and streams.
40cm tall. Aug.-Oct.

*Close-up
of flower*

➡ COMMON FUMITORY

Creeping plant with
much-divided, feathery
leaves. Tiny flowers are
tube-shaped and tipped
with purple. Cultivated
land. 30cm tall. May-Oct.

➡ SAND SPURREY

Spreading, mat-forming plant with sticky, hairy stems. Narrow, grey-green leaves end in a stiff point. Sandy places. 10cm tall. May-Sept.

Seed with hairy "parachute"

⬅ ROSEBAY WILLOWHERB

Also called Fireweed. Tall, erect plant with spikes of pink flowers. Long, narrow leaves. Common on waste ground. 90cm tall. July-Sept.

➡ HERB ROBERT

Spreading plant with a strong smell. The flowers droop at night and in bad weather. Leaves are red in autumn. Woods and hedgebanks. 40cm tall. May-Sept.

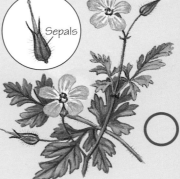

Close-up of flower

Sepals

93

PINK FLOWERS

Look for these flowers on heaths and moors.

Close-up
of flower

► HEATHER or LING

Shrubby plant with small, narrow leaves. Grows on heaths and moors. Leafy spikes of pink or white flowers. 20cm tall. July-Sept.

► BELL HEATHER

Like Heather, but taller. Thin, needle-like leaves and clusters of bell-shaped, pink flowers. Dry heaths and moors. 30cm tall. July-Aug.

Close-up
of flower

The berries
are edible

◄ BILBERRY

Small shrub with oval leaves. Drooping, bell-shaped, green-pink flowers. Heaths, moors and woods. 40cm tall. April-June.

Look for these flowers in
dry, grassy places.

Close-up
of flower
(top) and
fruit
(bottom)

➡ SORREL
Erect plant. Arrow-shaped
leaves have backward-
pointing lobes. Branched
spikes of flowers. Leaves
are eaten in salads.
Pastures. 20-100cm tall.

Lobe

Close-up of
flower (top) and
fruit (bottom)

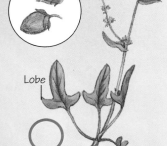

Lobe

◀ SHEEP'S SORREL
Smaller than Sorrel.
The lobes on the
leaves point upwards.
Dry places and heaths.
30cm tall. May-Aug.

➡ COMMON CENTAURY
Erect plant with rosette of
leaves at base and opposite
leaves on stem. Flowers close
at night. Grassland, dunes
and woods. 50cm tall.
June-Oct.

Opposite
pair of leaves

PINK FLOWERS

➡ RAGGED ROBIN

Flowers have ragged, pink petals. Erect plant wth a forked stem and narrow, pointed leaves. Damp meadows, marshes and woods. 30-70cm tall. May-June.

Bract (a kind of small leaf near the flower)

Grooved stem

⬅ KNAPWEED or HARD-HEAD

Erect plant with brush-like, pink flowers growing from black bracts. Grassland and waysides. 40cm tall. June-Sept.

Whorl of leaves

➡ HEMP AGRIMONY

Tough, erect plant with downy stem. Grows in patches in damp places. Attracts butterflies. Up to 120cm tall. July-Sept.

◀ DEPTFORD PINK

The clusters of bright
pink flowers close in
the afternoon. Pointed,
opposite leaves. Very
rare in Britain. Sandy
places. 40cm tall.
July-Aug.

*Close-up
of flower*

Fruit

➡ BLOOD-RED GERANIUM
or BLOODY CRANESBILL

Bushy plant with erect
or trailing stems. Deeply
divided leaves are round
and hairy. Hedgerows.
30cm tall. June-Aug.

Seed
pod

◀ RED CAMPION

Erect plant with a hairy,
sticky stem and pointed,
oval leaves in opposite
pairs. Woodland.
60cm tall. May-June.

PURPLE FLOWERS

◄ EARLY PURPLE ORCHID
Erect plant with dark spots on the leaves. Smells like cats. Look for the hood and spur on the flower. Woods and copses. Up to 60cm tall. June-Aug.

Tendril

➡ TUFTED VETCH
Scrambling plant with clinging tendrils. Climbs up hedgerows. Look for the brown seed pods in late summer. Flowers 1cm across. June-Sept.

Policeman's Helmet

Touch-me-not Balsam

◄ POLICEMAN'S HELMET
Also called Jumping Jack. Flowers look like open mouths. Ripe seed pods explode, scattering seeds when touched. Streams. Up to 200cm tall. July-Oct.

Policeman's Helmet is closely related to Touch-me-not Balsam

Look for these flowers in woods or hedgerows.

➡ FOXGLOVE
Erect plant with tall spike of tube-shaped flowers, drooping on one side of the stem. Large, oval leaves. Open woods. Up to 150cm tall. June-Sept.

➤ BATS-IN-THE-BELFRY
Erect, hairy plant with large, toothed leaves. Flowers on leafy spikes point upwards. Hedges, woods and shady places. 60cm tall. July-Sept.

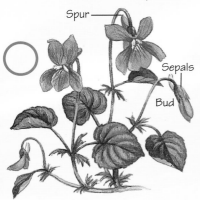

Spur

Sepals

Bud

⬅ COMMON DOG VIOLET
Creeping plant with rosettes of heart-shaped leaves. Look for the pointed sepals and short spur on the flower. Woods. 10cm tall. April-June.

PURPLE FLOWERS

Look in fields and other grassy places for these flowers.

➡ PASQUE FLOWER
Very rare in the wild, but grows in gardens. Hairy, feathery leaves. Purple or white flowers have yellow anthers. Dry, grassy places. 10cm tall. April-May.

Devil's Bit Scabious

Field Scabious

Field Scabious is a similar species

◀ DEVIL'S BIT SCABIOUS
Erect plant with narrow, pointed leaves. Flowers pale to dark purple. Round flowerheads. Wet, grassy places. 15-30cm tall. June-Oct.

Lobed leaves

Entire leaves

➡ FRITILLARY or SNAKE'S HEAD
Drooping flowers vary from white to dark purple. Chequered with light and dark purple. Damp meadows. 10cm tall. May.

You may see these
flowers on old walls.

➡ IVY-LEAVED TOADFLAX
Weak, slender stalks trail
on old walls. Look for the
yellow lips on the mauve
flowers. Flowers 1cm across.
Shiny, ivy-shaped leaves.
May-Sept.

*The stalk, with
flowers, does
not appear
very often –
usually you
will see only
the rosette*

◀ HOUSELEEK
A rosette plant with thick,
fleshy leaves. Dull red, spiky
petals. Does not flower
every year. Old walls
and roofs. 30-60cm
tall. June-July.

Rosette of leaves

➡ SNAPDRAGON
Erect plant with spike of
flowers. Long, narrow
leaves. Pouch-like flowers
are yellow inside. Old
walls, rocks and gardens.
40cm tall. June-Sept.

Fruit

RED FLOWERS

Look for these flowers on cultivated land.

Flowers may also be blue

➡ SCARLET PIMPERNEL
Grows along the ground. Flowers close in bad weather. Black dots under the pointed, oval leaves. Cultivated land. 15cm tall. June-Aug.

➡ POPPY
Erect plant with stiff hairs on stem. Soft, red flowers have dark centres. Round seed pod. Cornfields and waste ground. Up to 60cm tall. June-Aug.

Seed pod

Bud

Seed pod

⬅ LONG-HEADED POPPY
Like Poppy, but flowers are paler and do not have dark centres. Pod is long and narrow. Cornfields and waste ground. Up to 45cm tall. June-Aug.

← PHEASANT'S EYE
Rare cornfield weed with finely-divided, feathery leaves. The red flowers have black centres. 20cm tall. May-Sept.

Summer Pheasant's Eye (not in Britain) is a similar species

→ SWEET WILLIAM
Tough, narrow leaves and flat flower cluster. Mountain pastures and cultivated land in Europe. Gardens only in Britain. 60cm tall. May-June.

Close-up of flower

← WOOD WOUNDWORT
The leaves were once used to dress wounds. Spikes of dark red and white flowers in whorls. Smells strongly. Woods. 40cm tall. June-Aug.

WHITE AND GREEN FLOWERS

These flowers can be
found in woodlands
quite early in the year.

Split petals

➡ GREATER STITCHWORT
Look in woods and
hedgerows for this slender,
creeping plant. Grass-like
leaves in opposite pairs.
15-60cm tall. April-June.

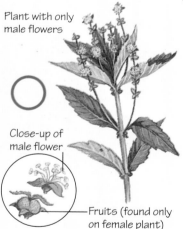

Plant with only
male flowers

Close-up of
male flower

Fruits (found only
on female plant)

⬅ DOG'S MERCURY
Downy plant with toothed
leaves in opposite pairs.
Strong-smelling. Male
flowers grow on separate
plants from female flowers.
Found in patches in
woodlands. 15-20cm tall.
Feb.-April.

Berry

➡ LILY-OF-THE-VALLEY
Grows in dry woods.
Broad, dark green leaves
and sweet-smelling flowers.
Red berries in summer.
Also a garden plant.
20cm tall. May-June.

➡ RAMSONS or WOOD GARLIC

Smells of garlic. Broad, bright green leaves grow from a bulb. Forms carpets in damp woods, often with Bluebells. 10-25cm tall. April-June.

Ramsons has long veins that run from one end of the leaf to the other

The large sepals look like petals

⬅ WOOD ANEMONE

Also called Granny's Nightcap. Forms carpets in woods. The flowers have pink-streaked sepals. 15cm tall. March-June.

➡ SNOWDROP

Welcomed as the first flower of the new year. Dark green, narrow leaves. Nodding white flowers. Woods. 20cm tall. Jan.-March.

WHITE AND GREEN FLOWERS

Look for these flowers in hedges or woods.

◤ JACK-BY-THE-HEDGE or GARLIC MUSTARD

Erect plant with heart-shaped, toothed leaves. Smells of garlic. Common in hedges. Up to 120cm tall. April-June.

Seed pod

➤ WILD STRAWBERRY

Small plant with long, arching runners and oval, toothed leaves in threes. Sweet, red fruits, covered with seeds. Woods and scrubland. April-July.

Fruits are smaller than garden strawberries

◀ WILD PEA

Very rare, scrambling plant with grey-green leaves. The seeds, or peas, are inside the pods. Climbs on thickets and hedges. Up to 250cm high. June-Aug.

Tendril

Pod

Look for these flowers in
hedges and waysides.

➡ WHITE BRYONY

Climbs up hedges with
spiral tendrils. The red
berries appear in August
and are poisonous. Large
underground stems, called
tubers. Up to 400cm tall. June.

Close-up of
female flower

Tendril

Berries

◀ COW PARSLEY

Also called Lady's Lace.
Look for the ribbed stem,
feathery leaves and white
flower clusters. Hedge
banks and ditches. Up
to 100cm tall. May-June.

Close-up
of flower

Fruit

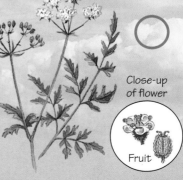

Close-up
of flower

Fruit

➡ HEDGE PARSLEY

Like Cow Parsley, but with
a stiff, hairy stem. Look for
the prickly, purple fruits.
Cornfields and roadsides.
60cm tall. April-May

WHITE AND GREEN FLOWERS

These flowers can be found in or near fresh water, such as streams and ponds.

Undersides of leaves are silvery-grey

➡ MEADOWSWEET
Clusters of sweet-smelling flowers. Grows in marshes, water meadows and also near ditches at the side of the road. Up to 80cm tall. May-Sept.

◀ TRIANGULAR-STALKED GARLIC or THREE-CORNERED LEEK
Smells of garlic. Drooping flowers. In damp hedges and waste places. 40cm tall. June-July.

The flower stem is three-sided

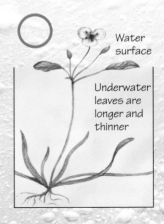

Water surface

Underwater leaves are longer and thinner

➡ FLOATING WATER PLANTAIN
Water plant with oval leaves and white flowers on the water surface. Look for it in canals and still water. Flowers 1-1.5cm across. May-Aug.

➡ WATER CROWFOOT

Water plant whose roots are anchored in the mud at the bottom of ponds and streams. Flowers (1-2cm across) cover the water surface. May-June.

These leaves are on the water surface

Fine, underwater leaves

⬅ WATER SOLDIER

Under water except when it flowers. Long, saw-like leaves then show above the surface. Flowers 3-4cm across. Ponds, canals, ditches. June-Aug.

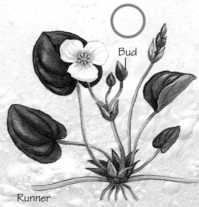

Bud

➡ FROGBIT

Rises to the surface in spring, and spreads with long runners. Shiny, round leaves grow in tufts. Flowers 2cm across. Canals and ponds. July-Aug.

Runner

109

WHITE AND GREEN FLOWERS

Look for these flowers in fields and other grassy places.

Clusters of small flowers

Close-up of single flower

Bracts

Fruit

Clusters of fruits

➡ WILD CARROT

Dense clusters of white flowers with a purple flower in the centre. Erect, hairy stem with feathery leaves. Grassy places, often near coast. 60cm tall. July-Aug.

Close-up of single flower

Fruit

◀ HOGWEED or KECK

Very stout, hairy plant with huge leaves on long stalks. Flowers are in clusters. Grassy places and open woods. Up to 100cm tall. June-Sept.

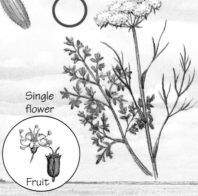

Single flower

Fruit

➡ CORKY-FRUITED WATER DROPWORT

Erect plant with large, much-divided, feathery leaves. Clusters of flowers. Meadows. 60cm tall. June-Aug.

White petals are sometimes tinged with pink

◀ DAISY
Small plant with rosette of leaves at base. Flowers close at night and in bad weather. Very common on garden lawns. 10cm tall. Jan.-Oct.

▶ WHITE or DUTCH CLOVER
Creeping plant, often grown for animal feed. Look for the white band on the three-lobed leaves. Attracts bees. 10-25cm tall. April-Aug.

White band

Runner

Look for the divided petals

◀ FIELD MOUSE-EAR CHICKWEED
Creeping plant with erect stems. Narrow, downy leaves. Grassy places. 10cm tall. April-Aug.

WHITE AND GREEN FLOWERS

Look for these flowers on cultivated land, waste land and waysides.

Close-up of flower

► COMMON ORACHE

An erect weed with a stiff stem and toothed leaves, both dusty grey. Cultivated land or waste places. Up to 90cm tall. Aug.-Sept.

Close-up of flower

► PIGWEED or COMMON AMARANTH

Erect, hairy plant with large, oval leaves. Large spikes of green, tufty flowers. Look for it on cultivated land. 50cm tall. July-Sept.

Single flower

Fruit

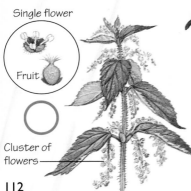

Cluster of flowers

◄ NETTLE

The toothed leaves are covered with stinging hairs. Dangling green-brown flowers. Used to make beer and tea. Common. Up to 100cm tall. June-Aug.

➡ GOOD KING HENRY

An erect plant with arrow-shaped leaves and spikes of tiny, green flowers. Farmyards and roadsides. 30-50cm tall. May-July.

Close-up of flower

Close-up of seed pod

Rosette of leaves

◀ SHEPHERD'S PURSE

Very common plant. The white flowers and heart-shaped seed pods can be seen all year round. Waysides and waste places. Up to 40cm tall.

➡ WHITE DEAD-NETTLE

Looks like Nettle, but the hairs do not sting. Flowers in whorls on the stem. Hedgerows and waste ground. Up to 60cm tall. May-Dec.

Note the "hoods" on the flowers

WHITE AND GREEN FLOWERS

➡ BLADDER CAMPION
Oval leaves in opposite
pairs. The sepals are
joined together, forming
a bladder. Grassy places
and hedgerows. 30cm
tall. June-Sept.

Calyx is smaller
than that of
Bladder Campion

When flowering
is over, fruit
grows inside
sepals (calyx)

◀ WHITE CAMPION
The erect stems and
the sepals are sticky
and hairy. The white
petals are divided.
Look in hedgerows.
Up to 100cm tall.
May-June.

➡ CORN SPURREY
Spindly plant with
jointed, sticky stems.
Narrow leaves in whorls
around the stem. Found
as weed in cornfields.
30cm tall. April-July.

Whorl of leaves

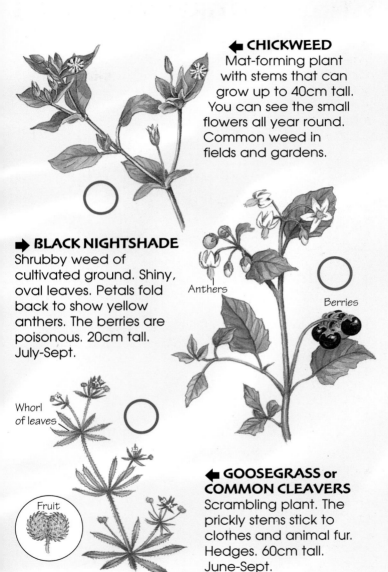

◀ CHICKWEED
Mat-forming plant with stems that can grow up to 40cm tall. You can see the small flowers all year round. Common weed in fields and gardens.

➡ BLACK NIGHTSHADE
Shrubby weed of cultivated ground. Shiny, oval leaves. Petals fold back to show yellow anthers. The berries are poisonous. 20cm tall. July-Sept.

Anthers

Berries

Whorl of leaves

Fruit

◀ GOOSEGRASS or COMMON CLEAVERS
Scrambling plant. The prickly stems stick to clothes and animal fur. Hedges. 60cm tall. June-Sept.

WHITE AND GREEN FLOWERS

Look for these flowers in grassy places, on waste or cultivated ground.

Anthers

▶ RIBWORT PLANTAIN or COCKS AND HENS
Tough plant with narrow, ribbed leaves. Green-brown spikes of flowers have white anthers. Common. 20cm tall. April-Aug.

Anthers

Anthers are mauve at first, changing to yellow

▶ GREATER PLANTAIN or RATSTAIL
Broad-ribbed leaves in a rosette close to the ground. All kinds of cultivated land. 15cm tall. May-Sept.

Anthers

◀ HOARY PLANTAIN
Rosette plant with oval, ribbed leaves. Fine hairs on stem. White flowers have purple anthers. Common in grassy places. 7-15cm tall. May-Aug.

Look for these flowers on grassy or waste ground.

◄ YARROW

Common plant with rough stem and feathery leaves. Flat-topped clusters of flowers. Smells sweet. Was once used to heal wounds. 40cm tall. June-Aug.

➡ WILD CHAMOMILE or SCENTED MAYWEED

Erect plant with finely divided leaves. The petals fold back. Waste places everywhere. 15-40cm tall. June-July.

◄ OX-EYE DAISY or MARGUERITE

Erect plant with rosette of toothed leaves and large, daisy-like flowers. Roadsides and grassy places. Up to 60cm tall. June-Aug.

WHITE AND GREEN FLOWERS

➡ STARRY SAXIFRAGE
A rosette plant with shiny, fleshy, toothed leaves. Mountain rocks. 20cm tall. June-Aug.

Meadow Saxifrage

➡ MEADOW SAXIFRAGE
Downy, lobed leaves. Up to 40cm tall. Grassy places.

Starry Saxifrage

Rosette of leaves

Seed pods

⬅ ALPINE ROCK CRESS
Short, mat-forming plant with rosette of greyish-green leaves. Dense clusters of white flowers. Rocks on hills and mountains. April-June.

Close-up of flower

➡ PELLITORY-OF-THE-WALL
Plant with red stems and soft hairs. Tiny, stalkless green flowers. Cracks in rocks and walls, and hedgebanks. Up to 100cm tall. June-Oct.

PROTECTING WILD FLOWERS

Many wild plants that were once common are now rare, because people have picked and dug up so many. It is now against the law to dig up any wild plant by the roots, or to pick certain rare flowers, such as the Red Helleborine.

If you pick wild flowers, they will die. Leave them for others to enjoy. It is much better to draw or photograph flowers, so that you and other people can see them again. Also, be careful not to accidentally tread on young plants or break their stems.

Red Helleborine

The Pasque Flower is a rare plant in the wild

If you think you have found a rare plant, let your local nature conservation club know about it as soon as you can, so they can help protect it. You can get their address from your local library or look on the Web. There is a list of useful addresses and Web sites on page 123.

119

FLOWER NOTEBOOK

You could record everything you discover about wild flowers in a notebook. Draw one plant on each page. Note its height, and when and where you found it. Note down anything else you notice, like butterflies and insects feeding or laying eggs on it. Try choosing a particular area to study.

Find a place where plants grow undisturbed, like a churchyard or a grassy verge. Mark out a square metre of ground with sticks and string. Identify and count the flowers you see. Try to find out why these plants grow in the same area. Keep a record of how they change in different seasons.

PHOTOGRAPHING FLOWERS

Photographs make a good record of the flowers you spot. If you take photographs while spotting, put them in your flower notebook along with your drawings and notes about flowers.

If you are photographing a flower, try to keep the sun behind you. Make sure your shadow doesn't fall on the flower, though. Try lying on the ground and photographing the flower from below, so it is outlined clearly against the sky. To prevent a flower from being lost among grass and leaves, try propping a piece of card behind it to make a plain background.

Tall plants with large flowers usually look best in photographs

Include the stems and seed pods in your picture

USEFUL WORDS

This page explains some of the specialist words used in this book. Words that appear in *italic* text are defined separately.

anther - the top part of the *stamen*. It produces pollen.

bract - a leaf-like structure at the base of a flower or stalk.

bulb - a mass of thick, fleshy leaves which store food for a plant under the ground.

calyx - a name for all the *sepals* together.

carpel - the female part of the flower. It consists of the *stigma*, *style* and *ovary*.

corolla - all the *petals*.

filament - the stalk of the *stamen*. It supports the *anther*.

flowerhead - a cluster of small flowers. It often looks like a single flower.

nectar - a sweet liquid produced by some plants to attract insects.

ovary - the part of the flower where seeds are produced.

petal - a segment of the *corolla*, usually brightly coloured.

pollination - when pollen reaches the *stigma*.

runner - a stem that grows along the ground.

sepals - leaf or petal-like growths which protect the flower bud and support the flower once it opens.

spur - a tube formed by the petals of some flowers. It often contains *nectar*.

stamens - the male parts of the flower. Each stamen is made up of an *anther* and a *filament*.

stigma - the top part of the *carpel*. It receives the pollen when the flower is pollinated.

style - part of the *carpel*. It joins the *stigma* to the *ovary*.

tendril - a thin stem or leaf that helps a plant to climb.

tuber - a large, underground stem.

weed - a plant that grows on waste or cultivated land, often getting in the way of other plants.

CLUßS AND WEß SITES

If you have access to the Internet, you can find out more about wild flowers and conservation clubs on the Web sites recommended below. For links to these sites, go to the Usborne Quicklinks Web site at **www.usborne-quicklinks.com** and enter the keyword "spotters".

Internet safety

When using the Internet, please follow the **Internet safety guidelines** shown on the Usborne Quicklinks Web site.

WEB SITE 1 Find the plants that live in your local area by using the London Natural History Museum's postcode plants database.

WEB SITE 2 The Web site of the Royal Botanic Gardens, Kew, London, where you can read about the threatened plants appeal and other conservation programmes.

WEB SITE 3 A UK national wild flower centre that promotes the creation of new wild flower landscapes.

WEB SITE 4 Discover the plant life in different habitats around the UK.

WEB SITE 5 A good general Web site about studying wild flowers and conservation.

WEB SITE 6 Learn about conservation surveys and campaigns, and how you can help, on the UK Plantlife conservation charity Web site.

SCORECARD

The flowers in this scorecard are arranged in alphabetical order. When you spot a species, fill in the date next to its score. Rare species score more than common ones.

After a day's spotting, add up all the points you have scored on a sheet of paper and keep a note of them. See if you can score more points another day.

Species (Name of flower)	Score	Date spotted	Species (Name of flower)	Score	Date spotted
Alpine Rock Cress	20		Common Dog Violet	10	
Alternate-leaved Golden Saxifrage	15		Common Forget-me-not	10	
Barberry	15		Common Fumitory	10	
Bats-in-the-belfry	15		Common Meadow Rue	15	
Bell Heather	15		Common Monkshood	20	
Bilberry	10		Common Orache	5	
Bird's Foot Trefoil	10		Common St. John's Wort	10	
Bistort	10		Common Speedwell	10	
Black Nightshade	10		Corky-fruited Water Dropwart	25	
Blackberry	5		Corn Spurrey	10	
Bladder Campion	5		Cornflower	25	
Blood-red Geranium	10		Cow Parsley	5	
Bluebell	10		Cowslip	10	
Brooklime	10		Creeping Buttercup	5	
Bugle	10		Creeping Cinquefoil	5	
Chickweed	5		Creeping Jenny	15	
Common Centaury	10		Cypress Spurge	15	

Species (Name of flower)	Score	Date spotted	Species (Name of flower)	Score	Date spotted
Daisy	5		Hoary Plantain	5	
Dandelion	5		Hogweed	10	
Deptford Pink	25		Houseleek	15	
Devil's Bit Scabious	10		Ivy-leaved Toadflax	5	
Dog Rose	15		Jack-by-the-hedge	5	
Dog's Mercury	10		Knapweed	10	
Early Purple Orchid	15		Knotgrass	5	
Field Mouse-ear Chickweed	10		Larkspur	15	
Field Scabious	15		Lesser Celandine	5	
Floating Water Plantain	15		Lesser Periwinkle	15	
Foxglove	10		Lily-of-the-valley	15	
Fritillary	20		Long-headed Poppy	5	
Frogbit	15		Meadow Clary	20	
Furze	10		Meadow Saxifrage	20	
Golden Rod	10		Meadowsweet	10	
Good King Henry	5		Nettle	10	
Goosegrass	5		Ox-eye Daisy	10	
Greater Bindweed	10		Pasque Flower	25	
Greater Plantain	5		Pellitory-of-the-wall	15	
Greater Stitchwort	5		Pheasant's Eye	25	
Heather	5		Pigweed	10	
Hedge Parsley	15		Policeman's Helmet	15	
Hemp Agrimony	10		Poppy	10	
Herb Bennet	10		Primrose	10	
Herb Robert	10		Purslane	15	

Species (Name of flower)	Score	Date spotted	Species (Name of flower)	Score	Date spotted
Ragged Robin	15		Triangular-stalked Garlic	20	
Ramsons	15		Tufted Vetch	10	
Rape	5		Viper's Bugloss	10	
Red Campion	10		Water Crowfoot	10	
Red Helleborine	25		Water Soldier	25	
Ribwort Plantain	5		White Bryony	15	
Rosebay Willowherb	5		White Campion	10	
Sand Spurrey	10		White Clover	5	
Scarlet Pimpernel	10		White Dead-Nettle	5	
Sea Holly	15		Wild Carrot	10	
Sheep's Sorrel	15		Wild Chamomile	15	
Shepherd's Purse	5		Wild Pansy	10	
Silverweed	10		Wild Pea	20	
Snapdragon	5		Wild Strawberry	15	
Snowdrop	15		Woad	20	
Soapwort	20		Wood Anemone	10	
Sorrel	5		Wood Groundsel	15	
Starry Saxifrage	15		Wood Sorrel	5	
Stonecrop	10		Wood Woundwort	10	
Summer Pheasant's Eye	25		Yarrow	5	
Sweet William	20		Yellow Archangel	10	
Touch-me-not Balsam	25		Yellow Pimpernel	10	

INDEX

PART THREE
TREES

Part Three – Trees
Written by Esmond Harris (Royal Forestry Society)
Illustrated by Annabel Milne and Peter Stebbing.
Edited by Jane Chisholm, Ingrid Selberg and Sue Jacquemier
Designed by Nickey Butler and Andrea Slane
With thanks to Zöe Wray and Lucy Parris
Consultant: Derek Patch, Director, Tree Advice Trust
Additional illustrations by Aziz Khan
Picture acknowledgements: page 129 © Richard Hamilton Smith/Corbis;
pages 130-131 © Bob Krist/Getty one Stone; backgrounds pages 132-185
and 188-191 © Digital Vision; pages 186-187 © James Marshall/Corbis

CONTENTS

HOW TO USE THIS BOOK

This book is an identification guide to some of the trees of Europe. Take it with you when you go out spotting. Not all the trees will be common in your area, but you may be able to find many of them in large gardens and parks.

WHAT TO LOOK FOR

There are lots of clues to help you identify a tree – whatever the time of year.

Yew

Oak

Common Beech

In spring and summer, look at the leaves and flowers. In autumn, look out for fruits, and in winter examine twigs, buds, bark and tree shape.

CONIFER OR BROADLEAF?

The trees in this book are divided into two main groups: conifers and broadleaves.

Conifers have narrow, needle-like or scaly leaves, and their fruits are usually woody cones. Most conifers are evergreen, which means they keep their leaves in winter. Their shape is more regular than broadleaved trees.

European Larch

Broadleaved trees have broad, flat leaves and seeds enclosed in fruits, such as nuts. Most are deciduous, which means they lose their leaves in autumn.

English Elm

132

KEEPING A RECORD

Next to each picture is a description, as shown in the example below.

A circle is next to each tree's picture. Put a tick in it when you spot an example of the tree.

Circle for ticking

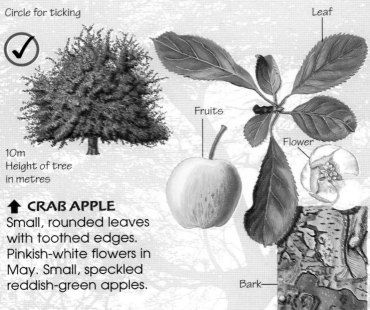

Leaf

Fruits

Flower

Bark

10m
Height of tree
in metres

⬆ CRAB APPLE

Small, rounded leaves with toothed edges. Pinkish-white flowers in May. Small, speckled reddish-green apples.

THE SCORECARD

Use the scorecard at the back of the book to give yourself a score for each tree you spot. A common tree scores 5 points and a very rare one is worth 25 points. If you like, you can add up your score after a day out spotting.

TREE	Score	Date spotted
Aleppo Pine	25	5/7/01
Aspen	15	20/7/01
Atlas Cedar	10	26/7/01

Fill in the scorecard like this.

THE LEAVES

Leaves will often give you the biggest clue to the identity of a tree. Beware, though, because some trees have very similar leaves. There are many different types of leaves. Some of the most common ones are shown here.

SIMPLE LEAVES

A leaf that is in one piece is called a simple leaf. Simple leaves can be many shapes: round, oval, triangular, heart-shaped, or long and narrow. The edges are sometimes spiky (like Holly) or toothed (slightly jagged). Some leaves have very wavy edges, called lobes.

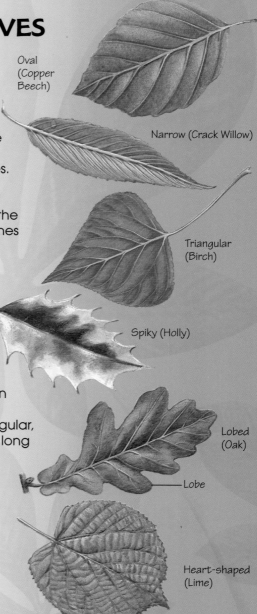

Oval (Copper Beech)

Narrow (Crack Willow)

Triangular (Birch)

Spiky (Holly)

Lobed (Oak)

Lobe

Heart-shaped (Lime)

COMPOUND LEAVES

A leaf that is made up of smaller leaves, or leaflets, is called a compound leaf.

Finger-like
(Horse Chestnut)

Leaflets

Feather-like
(Common Ash)

CONIFER LEAVES

Many conifers have narrow, needle-like leaves – either single, in small bunches, or in clusters. They can be very sharp and spiky. Some conifers, such as cypresses, have tiny scale-like leaves, which overlap one another.

Bunch of needles
(Atlas Cedar)

Pair of long needles
(Corsican Pine)

Short single needles
(Norway Spruce)

Scale-like leaves covering twigs
(Lawson Cypress)

135

FLOWERS AND FRUITS

All trees produce flowers that later develop into fruits, though some flowers are so small you can hardly see them. Most flowers have both male and female parts, but a few species, such as Holly, have male and female flowers on separate trees.

FRUITS AND SEEDS

Fruits contain the seeds that can grow into new trees. Broadleaved trees have many different kinds of fruits. Here are some of them.

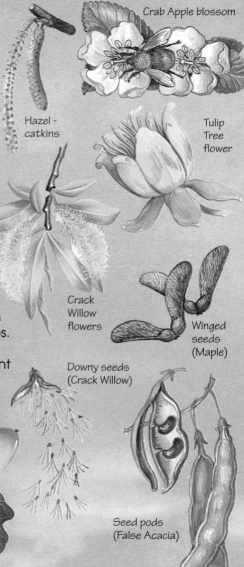

Crab Apple blossom

Hazel - catkins

Tulip Tree flower

Crack Willow flowers

Winged seeds (Maple)

Downy seeds (Crack Willow)

Acorn (Oak)

Seed pods (False Acacia)

Soft fruit (Cherry)

Soft fruit (Pear)

Crab Apple

Conker – (Horse Chestnut)

"Bobble" fruit (Plane)

Berries (Holly)

Cones in bunches (Norway Spruce)

Seed

Bract

Scale

Cone (Douglas Fir)

CONES
Conifers produce woody fruits called cones, made up of many overlapping scales containing seeds. At the base of each scale is a leaf-like part called a bract. Cones come in different shapes and sizes, and only some have visible bracts.

Scots Pine cone - seeds falling out

137

FINDING THE RIGHT TREE

The trees in this book are divided into conifers and broadleaves, with more closely related trees – such as all the oaks – grouped roughly together.

If you spot a tree you can't identify, but you know what type of leaf it has, you can use this chart to help you match it up with a tree in this book. The numbers show you where you'll find the illustration.

BROADLEAVES
Simple

Unlobed leaves

Common Alder......................164	Silver Birch............................174
Common Beech 171	Common Pear.........................172
Southern Beech..................170	Holly 182
Crab Apple.............................172	Aspen.....................................166
Holm Oak...............................161	Western Balsam Poplar....167
Whitebeam.............................165	Goat Willow 169
Black Italian Poplar............166	White Willow..........................170
Lombardy Poplar 168	Silver Lime...............................176
Crack Willow 169	Wych Elm...............................177
Common Lime 176	Wild Cherry...........................179
English Elm............................177	Black Mulberry....................180
Sweet Chestnut..................178	Cork Oak................................162
Bird Cherry 179	Whitebeam.............................165
Grey Alder..............................164	Blackthorn.............................174
Hornbeam 171	Magnolia.................................185

Lobed leaves

English Oak............................160	Sessile Oak............................160
Red Oak 162	Turkey Oak.............................161
White Poplar 167	London Plane.........................174
Sycamore 174	Norway Maple 175
Field Maple............................175	Tulip Tree................................184
Maidenhair Tree..................184	Hawthorn 173

Compound
Leaflets with a central stem

Common Ash.........163
Rowan 165
False Acacia 181
Manna Ash 163
Common Walnut.180

Finger-like leaflets

Horse Chestnut..178
Laburnum................181
Tree of Heaven 185

CONIFERS

Single needles

Needles grouped in 2s

Needles grouped in 3s

Needles grouped in 5s

Needles in more than 5s - Evergreen

Needles in more than 5s - Deciduous

Other conifers

Scale-like leaves

WHAT ELSE TO LOOK FOR?

Although the most obvious way to identify a tree is by its leaves, there are lots of other features to look out for too.

TREE SHAPE

You can sometimes tell a tree by its shape, especially in winter when many trees are bare. The leafy top of a tree is called its crown, and each type of tree has its own particular crown shape. This comes from the arrangement of its branches.

Cone-shaped
(Norway Spruce)

Narrow crown
(Lombardy Poplar)

Broad crown
(Oak)

TWIGS

Look closely at the way the leaves are arranged on the twigs. On some trees, they grow opposite each other in matching pairs. On other trees, the leaves are single and alternate from one side of the twig to the other.

The leaves of a Silver Birch alternate from one side of the twig to the other.

The leaves of a Horse Chestnut grow opposite each other in pairs.

BARK

The outside of a tree is covered in a hard, tough layer of bark, which protects the tree from drying out and from damage by insects and other animals. The type of bark a tree has can give clues to its identity too.

Silver Birch bark peels off in wispy strips that look like ribbons.

The bark of a Scots Pine flakes off in large pieces.

English Oak bark has deep ridges and cracks.

Beech trees have smooth thin bark, which flakes off in tiny pieces.

On the right is a cross-section of a tree trunk, showing the different layers, or rings. Each year, the trunk thickens by growing a new layer.

CONIFERS

⬇ SCOTS PINE

Short, blue-green needles in pairs, and small pointed buds. The bark is red at the top of the tree, and grey and furrowed below. The young tree has a pointed shape, becoming flat-topped with age.

Small bud

Short needles in pairs 5-7cm

Green pointed cone turns brown in second year

The bark flakes off in "plates"

Long bare trunk is red near top of tree

35m

Long needles in pairs 15-20cm

⬇ MARITIME PINE

Long, stout, grey-green needles in pairs. Long spindle-shaped buds. Long, shiny brown cones grouped in clusters. Rugged bark on a long, bare trunk.

Cones stay on tree for several years

Long bud

22m

142

Green cones
turn brown
with age

Paired
needles
12-15cm

20m

↑ STONE PINE
Umbrella-shaped tree
with a flat top, found
on the Mediterranean
coast. Long, dark green,
paired needles. Small
buds, and broad cones
with edible seeds.

Young
shoot

Prickly
scales

23m

↑ SHORE PINE
Tall, narrow, fast-growing,
with small cones in clusters.
Yellow-green needles in pairs
on twisted shoots. Scaly bark,
and sticky, bullet-shaped buds.

Paired
needles
4-5cm

CONIFERS

Branches grow at regular intervals

Rare in Britain

36m

Paired needles 12-18cm

Cones take two years to ripen

↑ CORSICAN PINE

Tall, fast-growing Mediterranean tree, found on rocky hillsides. Long, dark green, paired needles and onion-shaped buds. Large lop-sided brown cones. Blackish bark.

Young shoot

Paired needles

Rare in Britain

10m

Shiny, reddish cones stay on tree for many years

↑ ALEPPO PINE

Small, round-topped Mediterranean tree, with bright green, paired needles and small round buds. Its cones usually come in groups of two or three.

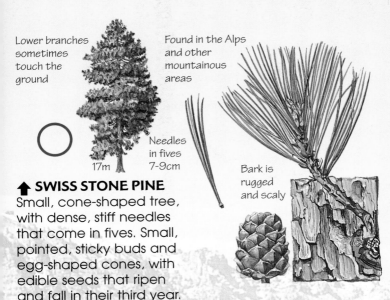

Lower branches sometimes touch the ground

Found in the Alps and other mountainous areas

Needles in fives 7-9cm

17m

Bark is rugged and scaly

⬆ SWISS STONE PINE

Small, cone-shaped tree, with dense, stiff needles that come in fives. Small, pointed, sticky buds and egg-shaped cones, with edible seeds that ripen and fall in their third year.

⬇ MONTEREY PINE

Slender, grass-green needles in threes. Large, pointed, sticky buds. Squat cones grow flat against the branches, staying on the tree for many years.

Needles in threes – about 10cm

Large, pointed sticky buds

Cones uneven at base

30m

CONIFERS

Needles 1-2cm

Cone scales are tightly closed

↑ NORWAY SPRUCE

Traditional Christmas tree. Regular conical shape, with prickly dark green needles and cones which hang down. Tiny bumps are left on the twigs when the needles are pulled off.

30m

Cones have papery scales with crinkled edges

Needles 2-3cm

35m

↑ SITKA SPRUCE

Narrow cone-shaped tree, with prickly blue-green needles and fat yellow buds. Small knobs left on yellow twigs when needles are pulled off.

Grey, scaly bark flakes off in "plates"

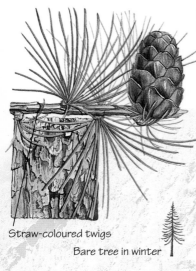

Straw-coloured twigs

Bare tree in winter

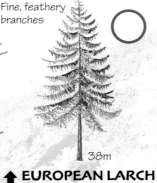

Fine, feathery branches

38m

↑ EUROPEAN LARCH

Bunches of soft, light green needles, which turn yellow and fall in winter, leaving small barrel-like knobs on twigs. Small, egg-shaped cones and reddish female flowers.

↓ JAPANESE LARCH

Bunches of blue-green needles, which fall in winter, leaving orange twigs. Pinkish-green female flowers and small, flower-like cones.

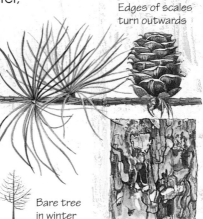

Edges of scales turn outwards

Bare tree in winter

The tree has thick branches   35m

147

CONIFERS

Young cones are green, turning plum-coloured with age

⬆ NOOTKA CYPRESS

Fern-like sprays of dull green, scale-like leaves grow on either side of the twigs. Plum-coloured cones have prickles on their scales. Cone-shaped crown.

25m

⬇ EUROPEAN SILVER FIR

Flat single needles, green above and silvery below. Flat, round scars left on twigs when needles drop. Cones shed their scales when ripe, leaving a brown spike.

Large, upright cones

Bracts showing

The twigs are smooth and the needles have notched tips

Rare in Britain, but common in central Europe

Very tall, narrow tree

40m

The needles have pointed tips

Bark flakes off in "plates"

30m

⬆ GREEK FIR

Shiny green, spiny-tipped needles all around the twig. Tall, narrow cones shed scales to leave bare spikes on the tree. Rare in Britain.

⬇ SPANISH FIR

Short, blunt, blue-grey needles all around twig. Cylindrical, upright cones, which shed scales when ripe, like those of the European Silver Fir.

The needles have blunt tips

The tree has a conical shape

28m

CONIFERS

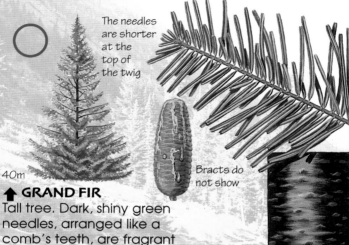

The needles are shorter at the top of the twig

Bracts do not show

⬆ GRAND FIR

Tall tree. Dark, shiny green needles, arranged like a comb's teeth, are fragrant when crushed. Whitish buds and small, upright cones.

40m

⬇ NOBLE FIR

Level branches and dense silver-blue needles, curving up. Enormous shaggy cones with down-turned bracts. Scales fall off, leaving tall spikes.

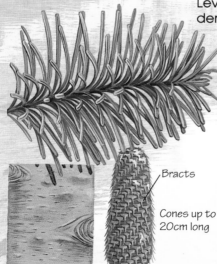

Bracts

Cones up to 20cm long

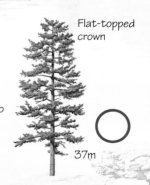

Flat-topped crown

37m

⬆ DOUGLAS FIR
Soft, scented needles. Copper brown buds with long points. Light brown hanging cones with three-pointed bracts. Bark is thick and grooved when old.

40m

Bracts

⬇ WESTERN HEMLOCK
Smooth, brown scaly bark, drooping branch tips and top shoots with small cones. Needles of various lengths, green above and silver below.

Tips of branches droop

Older cones are brown

Flattened needles

Young cones are green

35m

CONIFERS

⬇ WESTERN RED CEDAR

Small, flower-shaped cones and smooth, finely-furrowed bark. The twigs are covered with flattened sprays of scented, scale-like leaves.

Open cone

30m

Leaves are dark shiny green above and streaked white below

⬇ LAWSON CYPRESS

Sprays of fine, scale-like leaves, green and other colours. Small, round cones and smooth, reddish bark. The leader shoot (at tree top) often droops.

Small cones

Spray of scale-like leaves

25m

Cones are pale at first, dull grey when older

⬇ ITALIAN CYPRESS

An upright, narrow crowned, mainly ornamental tree. Small, dark, dull green, scale-like leaves, closely pressed to stem. Large, rounded cones.

Leaves are smaller than those of Monterey Cypress

15m

⬇ MONTEREY CYPRESS

Dense sprays of small, scale-like leaves and large, purplish-brown, rounded cones with knobs on scales. Column-shaped, becoming flat-topped when old. The bark is often peeling.

Leaves are lemon scented when crushed

25m

Peeling bark

Knob

153

CONIFERS

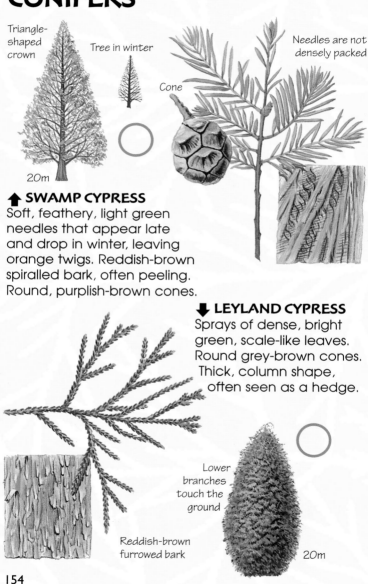

Triangle-shaped crown

Tree in winter

Cone

20m

Needles are not densely packed

⬆ SWAMP CYPRESS
Soft, feathery, light green needles that appear late and drop in winter, leaving orange twigs. Reddish-brown spiralled bark, often peeling. Round, purplish-brown cones.

⬇ LEYLAND CYPRESS
Sprays of dense, bright green, scale-like leaves. Round grey-brown cones. Thick, column shape, often seen as a hedge.

Lower branches touch the ground

Reddish-brown furrowed bark

20m

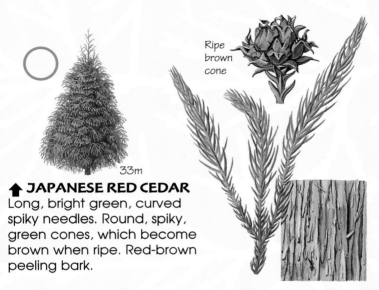

⬆ JAPANESE RED CEDAR

Long, bright green, curved spiky needles. Round, spiky, green cones, which become brown when ripe. Red-brown peeling bark.

Ripe brown cone

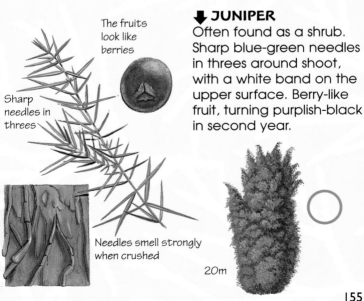

The fruits look like berries

Sharp needles in threes

Needles smell strongly when crushed

⬇ JUNIPER

Often found as a shrub. Sharp blue-green needles in threes around shoot, with a white band on the upper surface. Berry-like fruit, turning purplish-black in second year.

20m

CONIFERS

Wide spreading branches

15m

⬆ YEW

Seen in churchyards, as a wide, spreading tree or as a hedge. Red, berry-like fruit and wide needles, dark green above and yellowish below. Orange-brown flaking bark.

Needles and berries are poisonous

The cones are on long stalks

⬇ DAWN REDWOOD

Soft, light green needles, similar to those of the Swamp Cypress (see page 26), but larger, turning reddish in autumn. Bark is orange in young trees, flaking and furrowed in older ones.

The needles turn reddish in autumn

Bare tree in winter

20m

Needles parted
on either side
of the twig

⬇ COAST REDWOOD

Tall tree, with thick,
reddish, spongy bark.
Hard, sharp-pointed,
single needles, dark
green above and
white-banded
below. Small,
round cones.

33m

⬇ WELLINGTONIA

Tall, with soft, thick, deeply-
furrowed bark. Deep green,
scale-like, pointed leaves,
hanging from upswept
branches. Long-stalked,
round, corky cones.

Foliage hanging
from upswept
branches

Diamond-shaped
cone scales wrinkle
when they ripen

38m

CONIFERS

⬇ ATLAS CEDAR

Large, spreading tree with dark green needles, in bunches on the older shoots. Large, barrel-shaped, upright cones with sunken tops.

Sunken top

Needles are blue-green in the common garden variety, dark green in the wild

25m

Top not sunken

Cones are covered with sticky resin

30m

⬆ CEDAR OF LEBANON

Similar to Atlas Cedar, but without sunken tops on cones. Branches create flat platforms.

Leaves overlap each other

⬇ CHILE PINE

Unusual looking tree, with twisting branches, wrinkled bark, and a pole-like trunk. Stiff, leathery, triangular leaves with sharp points grow all around the shoots.

Broad, round crown

23m

⬇ DEODAR CEDAR

A tall cedar, with a pointed crown and soft, pale-green leaves, in bunches. Large, barrel-shaped cones have sunken tops.

The top shoot and branch tips droop

23m

BROADLEAVED TREES

Tall acorns on long stalks

Acorn cup

Lobe

⬆ ENGLISH OAK
Broad-crowned tree
with many large
branches growing
upwards from the same
point. Leaves have short
stalks and ear-shaped
lobes at the base.

23m

⬇ SESSILE OAK
Thick, dark, long-stalked
leaves tapering to the
base. Branches grow
from the stem at different
levels and point up in a
narrow crown.

All veins go to
tips of lobes

Acorn more rounded
than English oak

Acorn
often
stalkless

21m

⬇ HOLM OAK

Ornamental tree with a broad dense crown. Shiny, evergreen leaves, greyish-green beneath, sometimes with shallow teeth like Holly.

Teeth

Evergreen leaves

Small acorn, almost covered by cup

20m

⬇ TURKEY OAK

Leaves unevenly lobed. Whiskers on buds and at base of leaves. Acorns ripen in second autumn. Acorn cups mossy and stalkless.

Acorn cup is mossy

25m

161

BROADLEAVED TREES

16m

Twisted trunk and branches

⬆ CORK OAK

Common in southern Europe, but extremely rare in Britain. Smaller than other oaks, it has thick, corky, whitish bark and shiny, evergreen leaves with wavy edges.

Acorn

Cork is obtained from the bark

⬇ RED OAK

Smooth, silvery bark, and squat acorns in shallow cups that ripen in second year. Large leaves, with bristly-tipped lobes, turn reddish brown in autumn.

Leaves turn reddish in autumn

Acorn

20m

162

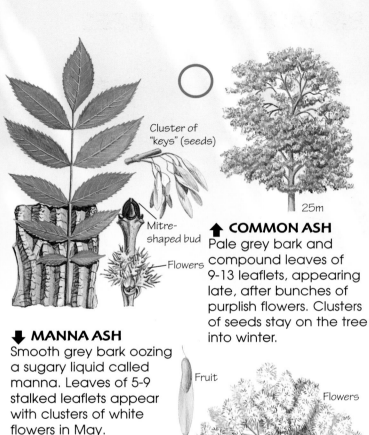

Cluster of "keys" (seeds)

Mitre-shaped bud

Flowers

⬆ COMMON ASH
Pale grey bark and compound leaves of 9-13 leaflets, appearing late, after bunches of purplish flowers. Clusters of seeds stay on the tree into winter.

25m

⬇ MANNA ASH
Smooth grey bark oozing a sugary liquid called manna. Leaves of 5-9 stalked leaflets appear with clusters of white flowers in May.

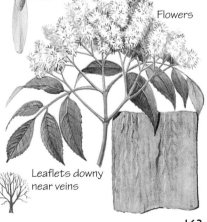

Fruit

Flowers

Leaflets downy near veins

20m

BROADLEAVED TREES

Leaf has
notched tip

Ripe brown,
woody cone

12m

⬆ COMMON ALDER
Rounded leaves fall in
late autumn. Reddish
catkins and small, brown,
woody cones. Sticky
young twigs and leaves.
Often found near water.

⬇ GREY ALDER
Fast-growing, with catkins
and fruit like the Common
Alder. Pointed oval leaves,
with sharp-toothed
edges, soft and
grey beneath.

Green fruits
ripen into brown,
woody "cones"

14m

One flower
(from a
cluster)

Leaves with
toothed
edges

7m

▲ ROWAN

Often grows alone on
mountains. Tooth-edged
compound leaves, smaller
than those of Common
Ash. Clusters of creamy-
white flowers in May, and
red berries in August.

Leaves turn
red in autumn

↓ WHITEBEAM

Flowers and berries similar
to Rowan, but ripening
later. Large oval leaves,
with toothed edges, dark
green above, white and
furry underneath.

Berries

8m

BROADLEAVED TREES

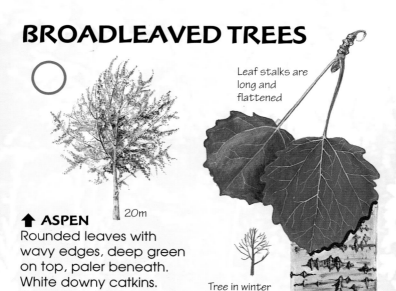

Leaf stalks are long and flattened

⬆ ASPEN

Rounded leaves with wavy edges, deep green on top, paler beneath. White downy catkins. Grey bark with large irregular markings. Often found growing in thickets.

Tree in winter

⬇ BLACK ITALIAN POPLAR

Dark green, triangular, pointed leaves appearing late. Red catkins and deeply furrowed bark. Trunk and crown often lean away from the wind.

Tree in winter

25m

Lower leaves are less lobed

Wavy edges

Underside of leaf

Diamond-shaped marks on young bark

20m

⬆ WHITE POPLAR

Five-lobed leaves, downy white underneath, so the crown looks white. Lower bark is dark and rugged; upper bark, pale grey, with diamond shapes on young trees. Tree often leans slightly.

⬇ WESTERN BALSAM POPLAR

Large, triangular, pointed leaves, very pale underneath. Sticky and sweet-smelling buds and young leaves. Long purplish catkins and white fluffy seeds.

Underside of leaf

35m

167

BROADLEAVED TREES

Leaf shape varies slightly

28m

↑ LOMBARDY POPLAR
Tall, narrow tree, often found along roadsides in mainland Europe. Pointed, triangular leaves, furrowed bark, and branches that grow upwards from the ground.

15m

↑ SILVER BIRCH
Slender tree with silvery bark and drooping branches. Small, diamond-shaped leaves, with toothed edges, and long "lamb's tail" catkins, in April.

Catkin

Silvery bark peels off in ribbons

Catkin "Pussy Willow"

Underside of leaf

↑ GOAT WILLOW

Also called Pussy Willow. Broad, rounded, rough, grey-green leaves. Silvery-grey upright catkins in late winter. Small bushy tree. Common on damp waste ground.

The crown shape varies

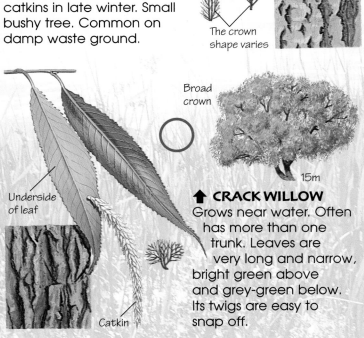

Broad crown

Underside of leaf

↑ CRACK WILLOW

Grows near water. Often has more than one trunk. Leaves are very long and narrow, bright green above and grey-green below. Its twigs are easy to snap off.

Catkin

BROADLEAVED TREES

Underside of leaf

Catkin

20m

⬆ WHITE WILLOW
Found by streams and rivers.
Long, narrow, fine-toothed
leaves, white underneath.
Slender twigs that are hard
to break. One variety with
trailing branches is known
as Weeping Willow.

Leaves
on short
stalks

Fruits

20m

⬆ SOUTHERN BEECH
Triangle-shaped crown,
and narrow, oval leaves,
with fine-toothed edges
and many obvious veins.
Deep green, prickly fruit,
and silver-grey bark.

Leaves are wavy-edged

Husk

Nuts

25m

⬆ COMMON BEECH

Tall tree with a spreading crown. Light green, oval leaves that turn copper brown in autumn. Smooth grey bark, and triangular nuts with hairy husks.

10m

Cluster of green winged fruits

⬆ HORNBEAM

Sharp-toothed, oval leaves. In autumn, clusters of three-pronged, leaf-like wings hold nuts. Smooth, grey bark is fluted, or rippled.

BROADLEAVED TREES

⬇ CRAB APPLE

Small, bushy tree, found in hedges. Rounded leaves with toothed edges. Pinkish-white flowers in May. Small, sour, speckled reddish-green apples that can be used in cooking.

Apple tastes sour even when ripe

10m

⬇ COMMON PEAR

Found in woods and hedgerows. Large, white flowers in April. Small pears that are gritty to eat. Small, dark green leaves, with finely toothed edges and long stalks.

Pear is golden when ripe

15m

5m

⬆ BLACKTHORN
Small tree, with oval leaves. Foamy, white flowers on bare twigs in March. Small, blue-black fruit, called sloes, in September.

Berries are called haws

8m

⬆ HAWTHORN
Shiny, deep-lobed, dark green leaves and thorny twigs. Clusters of small, white flowers in May, and dark red berries. Rounded crown.

BROADLEAVED TREES

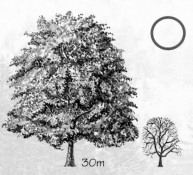

30m

⬆ LONDON PLANE
Large, broad leaves in
pairs, with pointed lobes.
Spiny "bobble" fruits hang
all winter. Flaking bark,
leaving yellowish patches.
Often found in towns.

Fruit

Leaves have
toothed edges

20m

Seeds spin
as they fall

⬆ SYCAMORE
Large spreading tree has
dark green leathery leaves
with toothed edges and
five lobes. Paired, right-
angled, winged seeds.
Smooth brown bark,
becoming scaly.

↑ NORWAY MAPLE

Light green, thin leaves, with bristle-tipped lobes and teeth. Wide-angled, paired seeds and finely-furrowed, grey bark.

15m

Pairs of seeds spin as they fall

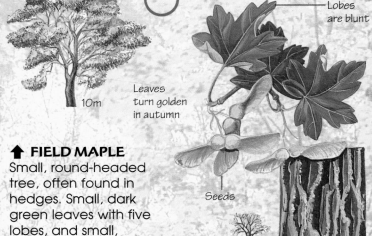

Lobes are blunt

Leaves turn golden in autumn

10m

Seeds

↑ FIELD MAPLE

Small, round-headed tree, often found in hedges. Small, dark green leaves with five lobes, and small, reddish, winged seeds.

BROADLEAVED TREES

Broad crown

25m

⬆ COMMON LIME
Heart-shaped leaves
with toothed edges.
Yellowish-green,
scented flowers in July.
Small, round, hard,
grey-green fruits hang
from a leafy wing.

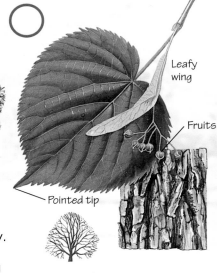

Leafy wing

Fruits

Pointed tip

⬇ SILVER LIME
Like the Common Lime,
but with a more rounded
crown. Dark green leaves,
silvery-grey below. Fruits
hang from a leafy wing.

Leafy wing

Fruits

Rounded crown

20m

Tall, narrow crown often has uneven shape

Now rare in Britain

30m

Flowers

Uneven base

Seed

Short point

▲ ENGLISH ELM
Rough, oval leaves with double-toothed edges and uneven bases. Clusters of red flowers appear before leaves.

▼ WYCH ELM
Like the English Elm, but has a round, even crown, larger, rougher, stalkless leaves, and larger seeds. Now very rare in Britain.

Uneven base

Seed

Clusters of red flowers

20m

BROADLEAVED TREES

⬇ HORSE CHESTNUT

Has compound leaves. "Candles" of white or pink flowers in May. Brown, inedible "conkers" are found inside green, spiny cases.

Upright "candle" of flowers

Leaflet

Tree in bloom

25m

Conker (fruit)

⬇ SWEET CHESTNUT

Long, narrow leaves with saw-toothed edges. Bark sometimes spiral-furrowed. Clusters of edible brown chestnuts in prickly cases.

Male flowers

Female flower

20m

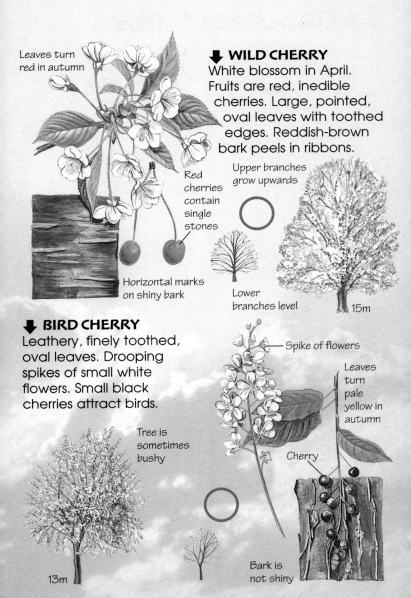

Leaves turn red in autumn

⬇ WILD CHERRY
White blossom in April. Fruits are red, inedible cherries. Large, pointed, oval leaves with toothed edges. Reddish-brown bark peels in ribbons.

Red cherries contain single stones

Upper branches grow upwards

Horizontal marks on shiny bark

Lower branches level

15m

⬇ BIRD CHERRY
Leathery, finely toothed, oval leaves. Drooping spikes of small white flowers. Small black cherries attract birds.

Spike of flowers

Leaves turn pale yellow in autumn

Tree is sometimes bushy

Cherry

13m

Bark is not shiny

179

BROADLEAVED TREES

Unripe fruit

Ripe fruit

Young fruits

25m

↑ BLACK MULBERRY

Rough, heart-shaped leaves with toothed edges. Blackish-red berries. Short trunk, twisted branches. Flowers in short spikes.

Smooth, green case containing edible walnut

Young fruit

↓ COMMON WALNUT

Broad crown. Smooth, grey bark, with some cracks. Compound leaves of 7-9 toothed leaflets, and hollow twigs.

Leaves are bronze when they first open, turning green later

20m

20m

↑ FALSE ACACIA

Smooth-edged compound leaves of many small leaflets. Hanging clusters of white flowers in June. Seeds in pods. Pairs of sharp thorns on twigs. Often has several trunks.

Smooth-edged leaflet

Deeply furrowed bark

Leaflets are soft and hairy

↓ LABURNUM

Leaf made up of three leaflets. Hanging clusters of yellow flowers. Poisonous seeds in twisted brown pods. Smooth green-brown bark.

Young seed-pods are green

Tree in bloom (May–June)

7m

181

BROADLEAVED TREES

↓ HOLLY
Small tree with shiny, dark, evergreen leaves that have thorny prickles. Small, white flowers. Round red berries. Smooth grey-green bark.

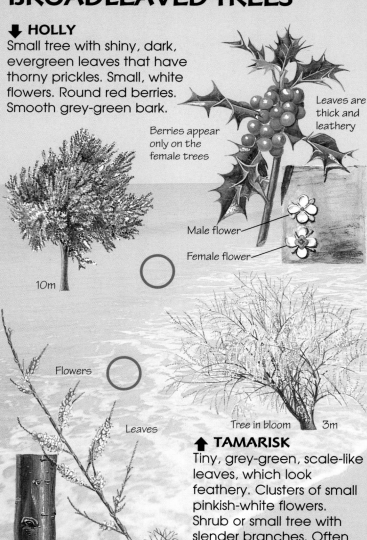

Berries appear only on the female trees

Leaves are thick and leathery

Male flower —

Female flower —

10m

Flowers

Leaves

Twig

Tree in bloom   3m

↑ TAMARISK
Tiny, grey-green, scale-like leaves, which look feathery. Clusters of small pinkish-white flowers. Shrub or small tree with slender branches. Often found near the sea.

Edible fruits are oily with hard stones

○

(Not in Britain)

10m

⬆ COMMON OLIVE

Small Mediterranean tree with a twisted trunk and narrow evergreen leaves in pairs. Clusters of small whitish flowers. Fleshy green fruit ripens to black.

⬇ EUROPEAN FAN PALM

Large, fan-shaped leaves made up of 12-15 stiff, pointed parts. Large clusters of small flowers and fruits. In the wild, it forms trunkless clumps of leaves.

Rare in Britain

○

Tall trunk only in planted trees

4m

Hairy trunk

BROADLEAVED TREES

20m

Squared lobe

Cone-like fruit

⬆ TULIP TREE
Smooth, four-lobed leaves, golden in autumn. Large tulip-like flowers in June. Upright, brown, cone-like fruits.

Flower

Cleft

⬇ MAIDENHAIR TREE
Tall, slender tree. Double-lobed, fan-shaped leaves with deep cleft, bright yellow in autumn. Female trees have hanging fruit, but male trees are more common.

Maidenhair Tree is neither a conifer nor a broadleaved tree. It is in a group of its own

Fruit looks like a small plum

23m

↑ MAGNOLIA
Wide, spreading tree.
Large white flowers on
naked twigs in March.
Large, smooth, dark green,
oval leaves appear later.

10m

Winged fruits ripen from
green to reddish-brown

Smooth grey-brown
bark with white streaks

22m

↑ TREE OF HEAVEN
Large compound leaves
made up of 5-20 pairs of
stalked leaflets. Large
clusters of greenish flowers
in July, followed by clusters
of winged fruits.

IDENTIFYING WINTER BUDS

Most broadleaved trees have no leaves in winter, but you can identify them by their winter buds. These contain the next set of shoots, leaves and flowers.

Use the pictures on the right to help you identify common trees by their buds and twigs. Look for:
• The shape, size and colour of the bud and twig.
• The position of the buds on the twig – in pairs, single, or alternate.
• The texture – the bud could be hairy, scaly, or even sticky.

False Acacia

Small buds with thorns at base, on grey, crooked, ribbed twigs

English Elm

Pointed, hairy, chocolate-brown buds on stout twigs

Ash

Large, black opposite buds on silver-grey twigs

Turkey Oak

Clusters of small, brown, whiskered, alternate buds

Common Alder

Alternate, stalked purple buds, often with male catkins

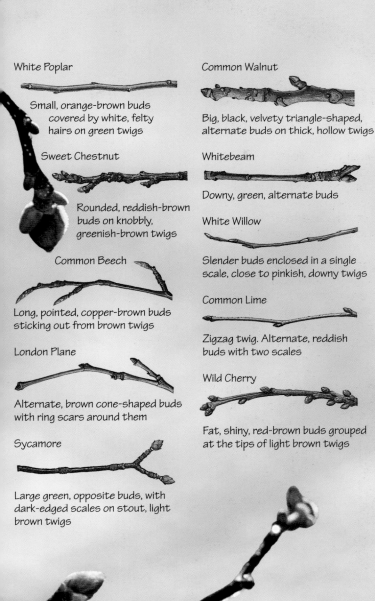

White Poplar

Small, orange-brown buds covered by white, felty hairs on green twigs

Sweet Chestnut

Rounded, reddish-brown buds on knobbly, greenish-brown twigs

Common Beech

Long, pointed, copper-brown buds sticking out from brown twigs

London Plane

Alternate, brown cone-shaped buds with ring scars around them

Sycamore

Large green, opposite buds, with dark-edged scales on stout, light brown twigs

Common Walnut

Big, black, velvety triangle-shaped, alternate buds on thick, hollow twigs

Whitebeam

Downy, green, alternate buds

White Willow

Slender buds enclosed in a single scale, close to pinkish, downy twigs

Common Lime

Zigzag twig. Alternate, reddish buds with two scales

Wild Cherry

Fat, shiny, red-brown buds grouped at the tips of light brown twigs

SCORECARD

The trees on this scorecard are arranged in alphabetical order. Fill in the date on which you spot a tree beside its name. A common tree scores 5 points, and a rare one is worth 25. After a day's spotting, add up all the points you have scored on a sheet of paper and keep a record of them. Can you score more points another day?

TREE	Score	Date spotted	TREE	Score	Date spotted
Aleppo Pine	25		Corsican Pine	10	
Aspen	15		Crab Apple	10	
Atlas Cedar	10		Crack Willow	15	
Bird Cherry	10		Dawn Redwood	20	
Black Italian Poplar	10		Deodar Cedar	10	
Black Mulberry	20		Douglas Fir	5	
Blackthorn	5		English Elm	25	
Cedar of Lebanon	10		English Oak	5	
Chile Pine	10		European Fan Palm	25	
Coast Redwood	15		European Larch	5	
Common Alder	5		European Silver Fir	10	
Common Ash	5		False Acacia	10	
Common Beech	5		Field Maple	15	
Common Lime	10		Goat Willow	5	
Common Olive	25		Grand Fir	15	
Common Pear	20		Greek Fir	20	
Common Walnut	10		Grey Alder	15	
Cork Oak	25		Hawthorn	5	

TREE	Score	Date spotted	TREE	Score	Date spotted
Holly	5		Scots Pine	5	
Holm Oak	10		Sessile Oak	5	
Hornbeam	10		Shore Pine	10	
Horse Chestnut	5		Silver Birch	5	
Italian Cypress	20		Silver Lime	20	
Japanese Larch	10		Sitka Spruce	10	
Japanese Red Cedar	15		Southern Beech	20	
Juniper	15		Spanish Fir	20	
Laburnum	5		Stone Pine	25	
Lawson Cypress	5		Swamp Cypress	20	
Leyland Cypress	5		Swiss Stone Pine	25	
Lombardy Poplar	10		Sycamore	5	
London Plane	5		Tamarisk	15	
Magnolia	15		Tree of Heaven	20	
Maidenhair Tree	20		Tulip Tree	20	
Manna Ash	15		Turkey Oak	10	
Maritime Pine	15		Wellingtonia	10	
Monterey Cypress	15		Western Balsam Poplar	10	
Monterey Pine	15		Western Hemlock	10	
Noble Fir	10		White Poplar	10	
Nootka Cypress	20		White Willow	10	
Norway Maple	10		Whitebeam	10	
Norway Spruce	5		Wild Cherry	5	
Red Oak	10		Wych Elm	25	
Rowan	5		Yew	5	

GOING FURTHER

If you have access to the Internet, you can find lots of information about trees online, and there are conservation societies that you can join. For links to these sites, go to the Usborne Quicklinks Web site at **www.usborne-quicklinks.com** and enter the keyword "spotters".

Internet safety

When using the Internet, please follow the **Internet safety guidelines** shown on the Usborne Quicklinks Web site.

WEB SITE 1 Find information about conservation on the Web site of the Wildlife Trusts, the UK's leading conservation society. There are ideas for ways to get involved and links to local conservation societies.
The Wildlife Trusts
The Kiln, Waterside, Mather Road,
Newark, Notts NG24 1WT

WEB SITE 2 On the Royal Forestry Society's Web site you can search an archive of British trees, and read about the Tree Aid scheme to plant trees in Africa.
The Royal Forestry Society
102 High Street, Tring,
Herts, HP23 4AF

WEB SITE 3 Join Wildlife Watch, the Wildlife Trusts club for young environmentalists.

WEB SITE 4 The Forestry Commission provides news about forests and woodlands, and conservation projects. You can look up the addresses of forest visitor centres in the UK, and find out where to see autumn colours in your area.
The Forestry Commission
231 Corstorphine Road,
Edinburgh EH12 7AT

WEB SITE 5 The Tree Council works to improve the environment by the conservation and planting of trees. The Web site has information about planting and caring for trees.
The Tree Council
51 Catherine Place,
London SW1E 6DY

WEB SITE 6 The Woodland Trust is dedicated to protecting Britain's native woodland. On their Web site you can find out about tree-planting events and conservation projects and read articles from their magazine.

The Woodland Trust
Autumn Park, Grantham,
Lincolnshire NG31 6LL

WEB SITE 7 The Royal Botanic Gardens at Kew has a unique collection of over six million specimens of plants and trees, covering 90% of the world's species. You can read all about their conservation work and collection, and find details of what's currently on show at the gardens.

The Royal Botanic Gardens
Kew, Surrey, TW9 3AB

WEB SITE 8 Find out about threats to forests on the WWF Web site.

WEB SITE 9 Read about the history of British woodlands since ancient times.

WEB SITE 10 Explore the Web site of the New Forest, "royal hunting ground of medieval kings", in the south of England. The site has useful maps, photographs and an informative factual history.

WEB SITE 11 A Web site all about British trees, with a useful illustrated guide.

WEB SITE 12 Fact files and information about timber use and forest management.

INDEX